THE DEVELOPING CHILD

Recent decades have witnessed unprecedented advances in research on human development. In those same decades there have been profound changes in public policy toward children. Each book in the Developing Child series reflects the importance of such research in its own right and as it bears on the formulation of policy. It is the purpose of the series to make the findings of this research available to those who are responsible for raising a new generation and for shaping policy in its behalf. We hope that these books will provide rich and useful information for parents, educators, child-care professionals, students of developmental psychology, and all others concerned with the challenge of human growth.

Jerome Bruner
New York University

Michael Cole
University of California, San Diego

Annette Karmiloff-Smith
Medical Research Council, London

SERIES EDITORS

The Developing Child Series

The Caring Child, by Nancy Eisenberg
Child Abuse, by Ruth S. Kempe and C. Henry Kempe
Children Drawing, by Jacqueline Goodnow
Children's Friendships, by Zick Rubin
Children's Talk, by Catherine Garvey
Daycare, by Alison Clarke-Stewart
Distress and Comfort, by Judy Dunn
Early Language, by Peter A. de Villiers and Jill G. de Villiers
Early Literacy, by Joan Brooks McLane and Gillian Dowley
  McNamee
Fathers, by Ross D. Parke
The First Relationship: Infant and Mother, by Daniel Stern
Infancy, by Tiffany Field
Mental Retardation, by Robert B. Edgerton
*Mind and Media: The Effects of Television, Video Games, and
  Computers*, by Patricia Greenfield
Mothering, by Rudolph Schaffer
The Perceptual World of the Child, by T. G. R. Bower
Play, by Catherine Garvey
The Psychology of Childbirth, by Aidan Macfarlane
Schooling, by Sylvia Farnham-Diggory
Sisters and Brothers, by Judy Dunn

The Learning-Disabled Child

Sylvia Farnham-Diggory

Harvard University Press
Cambridge, Massachusetts
London, England

Pages 203–204 constitute an extension of the copyright page.

This book is printed on acid-free paper.

Library of Congress Cataloging-in-Publication Data

Farnham-Diggory, Sylvia.
  The learning-disabled child / Sylvia Farnham-Diggory.
    p. cm. — (The Developing child)
  Includes bibliographical references and index.
  ISBN 0-674-51923-X. — ISBN 0-674-51924-8 (pbk.)
  1. Learning disabilities. 2. Learning disabled children. I. Title. II. Series.
RJ496.L4F37 1992
618.92'85889—dc20
91-35658
    CIP

Preface

The psychologists of my generation witnessed the birth of two major disciplines, developmental psychology and cognitive science. When I was in graduate school, these fields did not exist in their present forms. I learned about them, and contributed to them, during their formative years, and mine. I also worked and published in the field of abnormal child psychology. So, when Jerome Bruner first invited me in 1977 to contribute a volume to the Developing Child series, I chose a topic at the intersection of abnormal, developmental, and cognitive psychology: learning disabilities.

As I read through that earlier book I can see that I was trying to make sense, for myself, of a confusing picture. In this book I have tried to make sense of the field—still very confusing—for others. I try to provide guidelines especially for parents, teachers, and students, including those with an interest in research, each of whom may be seeing only a small part of the picture. Many parents, for example, will read this book in search of answers to the question "What's wrong with my child?" Many teachers, for answers to "How should I handle this child?"

For the past five years I have been addressing these questions in daily practice, as the director of the University of Delaware's Consultation and Assessment service (now discontinued because of budget cuts). I have met with many parents, teachers, children, and college students who believed that they, or someone they knew, might have a learning disability. I have dealt with school systems and learned about the sociopolitical forces that govern decisions to classify children as learning-disabled. I have directed research in educational policy, as well as in reading, dyslexia, attentional disorders, and schooling in general. I have been struck by the efforts that some teachers and other school professionals have made on behalf of individual children, and been frustrated by the closed-minded density of others. I have been able to view the entire spectrum of development, and in particular to study learning-disabled students of college age. The disability in these cases is much more sharply defined than it is in younger children, and clarifies what one should be looking for. This book, then, represents my attempt to make sense of the field not just for myself but for others, given my new understanding of their special points of entry and their vistas.

The book is still a personal one. It is written from a strong sense of concern for individuals who are seeking guidance through a confusing and often frightening domain. It describes the procedures that one consultation and assessment service worked out, through studying and experimenting with a number of alternatives, in a five-year effort to set clients on safe paths. It contains the broadest synthesis of current knowledge, and the clearest practical advice, that I know how to provide.

Acknowledgments

In 1985 I was asked to assume the directorship of two interconnected units in the College of Education at the University of Delaware. One was the Reading Study Center, a remedial clinic and training center, and the other was then known as the Psychoeducational Assessment Service. Eager to put theory into practice, I accepted happily, only to discover that, like most academics, I had no idea how to go about it. There began for me then a series of tutorials with school psychologists, special education teachers, school counselors, remedial reading tutors, learning disabilities specialists and psychometricians—only a few of whom there is space to mention here—in how such services actually worked. These patient and personally dedicated individuals include Marilyn Carver-Magnani, Laura Gordon, Marguerite Hoerl, Patricia Howe, David Johns, Chris Madden, Patricia Moeller, Marilyn Pare, Elizabeth Petrick, Lisa Schwartz, Rita Simon, and Neill Wenger. I thank them all warmly—on my own behalf, and on behalf of hundreds of clients—for their guidance, assistance, and insights.

I also thank Angela von der Lippe, of Harvard University Press, for encouraging me to bring out a new version of *Learning Disabilities*—so new, as it happened, that we decided to give it a new title—and for making the job so pleasant; Jennifer Snodgrass, my excellent editor; and Joseph Torgesen, for his careful scrutiny of the initial manuscript, and his many helpful comments. Above all, I thank Keith Heckert, of the University of Delaware's graphic services, for his skillful preparation of the art in this book.

Contents

The Learning-Disabled Child

1/ Compass Points

In American public schools, the rights of handicapped children to a free and appropriate education is a matter of law. The term "handicapped" has traditionally referred to the deaf, blind, physically disabled, and mentally disabled—including psychotic, retarded, and autistic children. Beginning in the 1960s, the term was extended to include a newly defined type of handicap called a "learning disability." As a matter of law, public schools must now provide free education that meets the special needs of learning-disabled youngsters.

Exactly what those needs are, and what is involved in correctly identifying them, is the general topic of this book. I begin with a description of the stream of events that typically results in the classification of a public school child as learning-disabled. These events have both formal (legally mandated) and informal aspects.

FORMAL CLASSIFICATION PROCEDURES

The process of classifying a child as learning-disabled typically begins when a teacher or a parent, or both, become dissatisfied with the child's performance in school. Testing (of the child, not of the teacher or the classroom, a point to ponder) is recommended. In the

1

public school system, there may be a long wait for such testing. Private testing (at the parents' expense) is an alternative, but the school may not be willing to accept the results of private testing. By law, public schools are required to accept certain test scores (IQ scores, for example) but not necessarily the private agency's interpretation of them.

States and school districts across the nation have different—sometimes very different—test requirements and diagnostic rules. In some states, children are classified as learning-disabled if they are reading a year or so below grade level. In other states, the classification is based on a sophisticated statistical measure of the discrepancy between the child's potential and her achievement on standardized tests.

Whatever the school rules, test data of various types are obtained. A conference is then convened, usually called a Child Study Team meeting, or an IEP meeting. IEP stands for Individualized Educational Program, and obtaining the parent's approval of that program is the object of the meeting. By law, a parent or guardian must attend the meeting, along with the person (usually a school psychologist) who reports the test results; perhaps a specialist such as a speech therapist or a reading supervisor; usually the child's classroom teacher; a special education teacher; and sometimes even the principal. At the meeting, the test scores are presented, the diagnosis is delivered, and the child's IEP is presented in written form.

The IEP specifies the new lessons the child will receive: extra reading instruction or a special science class, for example. Often the IEP presents the plan in terms of "behavioral objectives" for the child: "Billy will pass tests at the end of each social studies chapter at the 80 percent level." The special education staff plays a crucial role in these determinations.

Each school has one or more teachers who have credentials in special education. These teachers are in charge of what are usually called "resource rooms." Children can be assigned to resource rooms for tutoring or small-group instruction. In large elementary and secondary schools, the special education staff may also teach classes in social studies, science, reading, and so on. These will be small classes, so that students can receive more attention. Such classes nonetheless usually follow a standardized curriculum, although one less demanding than the regular curriculum. Thus the child's educational program may not be truly individualized. A guiding principle of special education placement is that the child must be placed in the least restrictive setting—mainstreamed in regular classes to the fullest extent possible. This is a matter of federal law.

When all the information about the child has been presented and discussed, and the parent is satisfied with the proposed program, the parent signs the IEP, and the meeting is adjourned.

On the face of it, the classification of a child as learning-disabled, and the prescription of the remedial program, appears to be properly documented and carefully thought out. What has been happening behind the scenes, however, may tell quite a different story.

INFORMAL CLASSIFICATION PROCEDURES

By the time a child is having classroom difficulties serious enough to be referred for testing, a stream of informal procedures will also have been set in motion.[1] The teacher will typically discuss the child with other teachers, the principal, the school psychologist, the special education teacher, and often with parents or guardians. Everyone tries to figure out the best way of handling the situation—to help the child, and, especially if the child is troublesome, to help the teacher. By the time test scores come in (usually months after the referral), concerned school personnel will have largely decided how to handle the problem. They will have decided, for example, that the child should be assigned to the resource room for special help with arithmetic because the special education teacher is known for her skills in helping children with arithmetic. For an obstreperous child, who makes it difficult for the teacher to devote adequate attention to the other children in the class, the main objective may be to get the child out of the class for the longest possible amount of time. Solutions may also involve problems that parents present. If a militant parent who considers himself an authority on reading will be placated by providing a child with supplementary reading instruction, then it may be provided, even though the teacher says the child is reading well. Of course the child will have to miss science class, because that's when the supplementary reading class is held, but that can't be helped. These solutions may not have evolved without controversy among staff members, and they may not be good solutions by some standards, but they are "minimax" solutions: they strive for the minimum discomfort and the maximum satisfaction all around.

Test scores therefore typically take their place within the framework of solutions that have already been worked out. There is often wide leeway in test choice and interpretation, and in how much of the data have to be reported. For the purposes of the IEP meeting, it is enough that the school diagnostician describes the problem and indicates that "tests" have verified it. In fact, the problem was identified long before the test data were obtained.

The IEP has often been worked out and written up in

advance of the meeting. This is actually against federal rules. The program for the child is supposed to be worked out at the meeting, in collaboration with the parents. But in this computer age, many schools automatically compile IEPs from lists of objectives that represent programs already in place. The child may join a group of students in a resource room, all of whom are receiving the same instruction, and all of whom therefore received the same IEP. I once saw a teacher, preparing for an IEP meeting, erase one child's name from an IEP, and write in another's—despite the fact that one child was retarded, and the other had a speech problem. Incidents of this sort are commonplace.

IMPLICATIONS

It is by no means a foregone conclusion that these informal, behind-the-scenes classification procedures are bad. The crucial issue is the quality of the school staff. The child may well have been provided with excellent services: The child has been considered, in depth, as an individual; his strengths, weaknesses, aspirations, and talents have been thoroughly discussed. A substantial amount of behind-the-scenes adjustment may have been made to shunt the child into a more appropriate program. The child may have been tactfully rescued from a teacher who was wrong for him, and placed in a new environment where he is more likely to thrive. The fact that test scores, classification criteria, and formal IEPs were contrived in order to legalize these decisions doesn't mean the decisions were wrong. So, why worry?

Well, there are several reasons to worry. First, an alarming number of children are misclassified as learning-disabled. By recent estimates, 80 percent of the children who are classified as learning-disabled should not have been.[2] Their families believe that something is wrong with their child's brain, when there isn't.[3] They believe that school personnel have come up with an authoritative diagnosis, based on test scores and expert judgment, when they haven't.[4] Parents are not told: "Look, the problem is that your child is in a class with an inexperienced teacher who doesn't know how to teach reading very well. But we'll offend the teacher and stir up union problems if we go on the record with that. The best way to get your child more competent instruction is to classify him as learning-disabled, which we have figured out a way to do, and assign him to a special education reading class." No one will say to a parent who is desperate for a child to attend college: "Your child just doesn't have the academic aptitude to keep up with the college-bound classes. Her SAT scores are not competitive. But we've figured out a way to classify her as learning-disabled, and that means she can take the SATs again, untimed, which should help offset her high school record." In this case, because the competitive situation is much worse in college, the school may be starting the youngster down a cruel garden path.[5] Sound judgments about a child's future must be made on the basis of accurate information, not on the basis of hopes and fantasies and romantic misconceptions engendered in part by a school's well-meaning efforts to find congenial solutions to immediate problems.

Second, the rare genuinely learning-disabled children—perhaps five out of every thousand children—are often lost in the misclassified crowd, and are not receiving the specialized education that they need and that federal law mandates. This is a direct violation of the children's legal rights. The informal classification procedures used by school personnel, however well meant, usually do not detect such children, especially if the children are well-behaved in class.

Third, these informal procedures seriously undermine research into the nature of learning disabilities. Millions of federal research dollars have been spent investigating the mental characteristics of children whom schools have classified as learning-disabled. But those classifications are based on diverse situational factors that are totally unknown to the researcher. There is no reason to assume that the children selected by these behind-the-scenes maneuvers will have any common characteristics, except, perhaps, that they are perceived by teachers and/or parents as not learning well in class.

Finally, misclassification of children has extensive economic implications. Once a child has been classified as learning-disabled, additional money is sent to the school district on that child's behalf. The exact amount varies, but it is quite substantial. At present, it is about seven thousand dollars per learning-disabled child per year. The money is not spent directly on individual children, but goes into a general budget to pay special education personnel, buy supplies, and so on. Thus there is a good deal of incentive for school districts to classify children as learning-disabled.

Additionally, there are now many private agencies that specialize in diagnosing, tutoring, or counseling students with learning disabilities. There are private (usually very expensive) schools and camps for students with learning disabilities. Learning disability is, in fact, a growth industry. (I have actually been contacted by financial advisors wanting to know if this or that remedial system would be a good investment for their clients.)

Hence, in the years since my earlier publication, the field of learning disabilities has exploded and—like any explosion—has gone out of control. This has been widely recognized, and new policies, intended to halt misclassifications, are being formulated. It is likely that within the next few years, the number of children that a district is permitted to classify as learning-disabled will be restricted to 2 percent of the total number of handicapped students. It will therefore become imperative for districts to develop objective, consistent criteria for detecting the genuinely learning-disabled child. My major reason for producing a new book on learning disabilities is to offer parents, teachers, school administrators, policy makers, and concerned taxpayers information that will help them think through the complex and sometimes acutely personal issues that converge on the question: Is this a learning-disabled child?[6]

The remainder of Chapter 1 will summarize current definitional, legal, and policy issues. To explain where these issues have come from, Chapters 2 and 3 will trace the early and recent history of the field. Chapters 4 and 5 survey what research is being done, and what we currently know. Chapters 6, 7, and 8 focus upon the primary tasks that learning-disabled children fail, especially reading, writing, and arithmetic. Chapter 9 comes to terms with these questions: How can we best identify genuinely learning-disabled children? What services do they need? And what services should be provided for those children who are being misclassified?

THE LEGALITIES OF LEARNING DISABILITIES

In 1976, the federal Education for All Handicapped Children Act was amended to mandate "free and appropriate" education for all handicapped children in public schools. This amendment is known as Public Law 94-142. Funds and "appropriate" educational programs were to be made available for these children. Each such child must be registered, by name, with the state and the federal government, as having a handicap, and as having consequent educational needs which cannot be met in a regular classroom. This registry is entirely confidential, but it is mandatory.

Children who are eligible for special assistance may be deaf, blind, motor-impaired, retarded, emotionally disturbed (this could mean disruptive, withdrawn, or psychotic), or learning-disabled. Learning-disabled children were defined as follows:

> Children with special learning disabilities exhibit a disorder in one or more of the basic psychological processes involved in understanding or in using spoken or written language. These may be manifested in disorders of listening, thinking, talking, reading, writing, spelling, or arithmetic. They include conditions which have been referred to as perceptual handicaps, brain injury, minimal brain dysfunction, dyslexia, developmental aphasia, etc. They do not include learning problems which are due primarily to visual, hearing, or motor handicaps, to mental retardation, emotional disturbance or to environmental disadvantage.[7]

In 1981, another definition was adopted by some agencies, but to my knowledge P.L. 94-142 has not yet been formally amended to include it. The new definition was intended to clarify some of the ambiguities. Whether or not it did so is still a matter of debate.

> Learning disabilities is a generic term that refers to a heterogeneous group of disorders manifested by significant difficulties in the acquisition and use of listening, speaking, reading, writing, reasoning or mathematics. These disorders are intrinsic to the individual and presumed to be due to central nervous system dysfunction. Even though a learning disability may occur concomitantly with other handicapping conditions (e.g., sensory impairment, mental retardation, social and emotional disturbance) or environmental influences (e.g., cultural dif-

ferences, insufficient or inappropriate instruction, psychogenic factors), it is not the direct result of those conditions or influences.[8]

P.L. 94-142 leaves specific procedures for classifying learning-disabled children up to individual school districts. Many use some type of aptitude-achievement discrepancy formula (described in Chapter 9). But some districts have used very different types of classification procedures, such as describing as learning-disabled any child reading below grade level (by a specified number of grades). Other districts use special tests, or special ways of interpreting standardized tests, in order to classify children as learning-disabled.

In all cases, the classification process is exclusionary: to be categorized as learning-disabled, the child must *not* fit into any of the other handicapped categories. IQ must be above 70 (otherwise, the child would be categorized as retarded); the child must not be deaf, blind, emotionally disturbed, or economically deprived. This has been a matter of controversy, because a learning disability can occur in conjunction with any of these other handicaps. But the exclusionary rule is not a philosophical judgment, it is a budgetary policy. If a child's primary disability is deafness, then funds for that child's special educational needs are to come from the budget for deaf children, and so on. Only if the child is not deaf, blind, retarded, poor, or emotionally disturbed can funds for his special needs be drawn from the budget for children with learning disabilities.

PREVALENCE AND COSTS

Overall, about 11 percent of all children enrolled in public schools receive special education services under P.L. 94-142.[9] Table 1 shows how this 11 percent is distrib-

Table 1. Special Education Population Trends, 1976–77 to 1985–86

	1976–77	1977–78	1978–79	1979–80	1980–81	1981–82	1982–83	1983–84	1984–85	1985–86
Number in eligible population (in 1000s)	44,322	43,566	42,549	41,632	40,969	40,096	39,655	39,144	38,561	39,353
Number served (in 1000s)										
Total special education	3,692	3,751	3,889	4,005	4,142	4,198	4,255	4,298	4,315	4,317
Learning disabled	796	964	1,130	1,276	1,462	1,622	1,741	1,806	1,823	1,862
Speech impaired	1,302	1,223	1,214	1,186	1,168	1,135	1,131	1,128	1,129	1,128
Mentally retarded	959	933	901	869	829	786	757	727	708	661
Emotionally disturbed	283	288	300	329	346	339	352	361	372	376
Other severely impaired[a]	353	342	344	345	337	314	273	277	302	294
Percent of total population classified as:										
Total special education	8.33	8.61	9.14	9.62	10.11	10.47	10.73	10.98	11.19	10.97
Learning disabled	1.80	2.21	2.66	3.06	3.57	4.05	4.39	4.62	4.72	4.73
Speech impaired	2.94	2.81	2.85	2.85	2.85	2.83	2.85	2.88	2.90	2.86
Mentally retarded	2.16	2.14	2.12	2.09	2.02	1.96	1.91	1.86	1.84	1.68
Emotionally disturbed	0.64	0.66	0.71	0.79	0.85	0.85	0.89	0.92	0.96	0.95
Other severely impaired[a]	0.81	0.79	0.82	0.83	0.83	0.79	0.69	0.70	0.78	0.75
Percent of special education population classified as:										
Learning disabled	21.5	25.7	29.1	31.9	35.3	38.6	40.9	42.0	42.2	43.1
Speech impaired	35.3	32.6	31.2	29.6	28.2	27.0	26.6	26.2	25.9	26.1
Mentally retarded	26.0	24.9	23.2	21.7	20.0	18.7	17.8	16.9	16.4	15.3
Emotionally disturbed	7.6	7.7	7.7	8.2	8.4	8.1	8.3	8.4	8.6	8.7
Other severely impaired[a]	9.5	9.1	8.9	8.6	8.2	7.6	6.5	6.5	7.0	6.8

Source: Data are for children ages 3–21 in the 50 states and District of Columbia; for 1976–77 through 1983–84, National Center for Education Statistics, *The Condition of Education* (Washington, D.C.: U.S. Department of Education, 1985), Table 4.1, p. 182; and for 1984–85 through 1985–86, Office of Special Education and Rehabilitative Services, *Ninth Annual Report to Congress on the Implementation of the Education of the Handicapped Act* (Washington, D.C.: U.S. Department of Education, 1987), Table 2, p. 5.

a. Other severely impaired includes children classified as hard of hearing, deaf, multihandicapped, orthopedically impaired, other health impaired, visually impaired, and deaf-blind.

uted among categories, and how the distribution has changed since 1977. The percentage of the special education population classified as learning-disabled doubled in ten years. In 1976–77, 21.5 percent of all handicapped children were classified as learning-disabled; by 1985–86, the percentage was 43.1. All but one of the other categories have decreased. The exception is emotional disturbance, which increased by only about 1 percent. Clearly, children who used to be classified as having other impairments were being classified as learning-disabled.

A year later (1986–87), the percentage of learning-disabled increased to 43.6, mentally retarded dropped to 15.0, and emotionally disturbed held steady at 8.7. The trend continues.

In terms of numbers, about 800,000 children were classified as learning-disabled in 1977. By 1986, the number was 1.9 million. The retarded group, on the other hand, decreased over the same time period by 298,000, and the other severely impaired group decreased by 59,000. In 1986–87 the same trends continued: the learning-disabled pool increased by an additional 53,760, and the mentally retarded decreased by 21,635.

Average costs for services provided for each child are shown in Table 2. These costs were obtained from five representative school districts—Charlotte-Mecklenburg Schools, in North Carolina; Houston Independent School District, Texas; Milwaukee Public Schools, Wisconsin; Rochester City School District, New York; and Santa Clara County Office of Education, California. The costs of services for children with physical and sensory impairments are the highest (the cost of a sign language interpreter, for example), but apply only to a very small number of children (4 percent of the special education population). The amount spent on the learning-disabled

Table 2. Allocation of Funds in Representative School Districts

Primary handicap	Mean expenditure in dollars	Percent of special education population	Percent of special education expenditures
Learning disabled	7,172	43	44
Speech impaired	5,414	27	21
Mentally retarded	7,853	15	16
Emotionally disturbed	8,204	11	13
Physically, hearing, visually, or health impaired	10,791	4	7

group averaged about $7000 per child. If this is close to the national average, and it probably is, then we should multiply 1.9 million by $7000 to arrive at something over 13 billion dollars being spent annually on services for learning-disabled children.

EFFECTIVENESS OF SERVICES

Most parents of children in special education programs say they are quite satisfied with their children's educational services, and most teachers say the children show improvement. But there are no national data available on exactly what has resulted, for each child, from the additional thousands that come into a district under that child's name. There are, of course, records of how the money was spent, and most of it goes into personnel. What exactly do these personnel pass on to the children? How much do the children actually improve from their own starting levels? In the absence of hard data, answers to such questions tend to be guided by one's general attitude toward the effectiveness of education generally, and toward social service policies.

It can be argued, for example, that American education

is in a sad state overall.[10] Only 4.9 percent of our population can read well enough to handle college-level material.[11] American children score lowest of all industrialized nations on science and math tests.[12] Getting handicapped children "up to speed," then, may not be getting them very far. Would we be better advised to use those billions to overhaul the education system generally?

It is quite possible to design a classroom program that welcomes individual differences among children, and that invites each child to make personalized contributions to exciting class projects. Such constructive, creative, cooperative classrooms easily incorporate handicapped children. It is only the competitive traditional academic classrooms that set apart, at the low end of many scales, the handicapped children. It is within the framework of competitive traditional academic classrooms that handicapped children fail, that teachers are driven to extrude children who don't fit in, and that special educators must try to teach survival skills.[13]

Another possibility would be to put the money into individual tutoring, which educational research has shown beyond doubt is the very best form of instruction.[14] Whatever gains learning-disabled children make may well be attributable primarily to individual attention. For $7000 a year, first-class tutors, paid at the rate of $30 an hour, could provide the child with an hour of tutoring every single school day, with extra left over for the summer. In that way, we could be absolutely sure that each dollar went into direct services for the child, rather than into personnel expansion, paperwork costs, and what are referred to as "cross-subsidies," where money allocated for one type of handicapped child goes into a general budget that can be used for other purposes.

From the social service standpoint, there are arguments over whether the money should go into education at all. Might it serve the nation better if it were put into urban renewal? Into rescuing children from social conditions that schools cannot begin to compensate for? How can an extra hour in a resource room compensate for growing up in a drug-ridden slum? To what extent is P.L. 94-142 making the liberals among us feel as if we're doing some good, when in fact we may be doing nothing more than helping to build a fat new bureaucracy?

In the conservative political climate of our day, such arguments are going to have an effect. Unless we can become much more precise about what a learning disability is, and much more cost-effective in remediating it, learning-disabled children are likely to be swept away in a muddy political backwash.

2/ Origins of the Field

Most writers begin their history of learning disabilities with the publication of Kurt Goldstein's book, *Aftereffects of Brain Injuries in War,* in 1942.[1] The book is cited because of the influence it had on Alfred Strauss, a neuropsychiatrist who was a refugee from Nazi Germany. Goldstein's general theme was that, even after the brain wounds healed, behavioral disturbances persisted. The implication, for Strauss, was that comparable disturbances in children's behavior could be attributed to brain injuries.

Strictly speaking, this inference was not logical, but it had two important consequences: it encouraged research into subtle forms of brain injury and into unsuspected causal mechanisms (anesthesia during childbirth, for example); and it helped mentally disabled children and their parents climb off the painful hooks of self-blame. Until the concept of brain injury was introduced, a child's bad behavior and failure in school were considered to be somebody's fault. But an accident to the brain was nobody's fault: parents and children could stop feeling guilty and set about seeking help.

From his base at the Wayne County Training School in Michigan, Strauss wrote a very influential book with Laura Lehtinen called *Psychopathology and Education of the Brain-Injured Child,* published in 1947.[2] It is important to realize that this book was about exceptional children. Such children, like mentally normal children, show wide individual differences in behavior. In trying to develop appropriate educational strategies, Strauss and Lehtinen grouped exceptional behavior into six categories. One was of special interest: exogenous brain damage, in which something external to the genetic developmental plan was responsible for the damage. So-called exogenous children were described as emotionally unstable, perceptually disordered, impulsive, distractible, and repetitive. This was behavior that Goldstein had also observed in his brain-injured soldiers. In children, it later became known as the Strauss syndrome.

There were two other influences on the Straussian characterization of a brain-injured child. One was the then current notion regarding equipotentiality of brain function. This term was introduced by Karl Lashley in 1929 and referred to the likelihood that one part of the brain could substitute for another.[3] Lashley showed that rats will become learning-disabled if one removes portions of their brains. However, the *location* of the extirpated piece did not seem to matter; what mattered was the *size*. The implication for Strauss was that it was not necessary to specify the location of brain damage in children in order to assert that brain damage had occurred. This was a curious bit of theoretical illogic, and another followed. Strauss seems to have concluded that because nonspecific brain injury could be shown to result in behavioral disorders, then behavioral disorders could imply nonspecific brain injury. He apparently believed that brain damage "was frequently the result of small, diffuse hemorrhages scattered throughout the brain."[4]

We now know that such neurological theorizing was a confused oversimplification. More sophisticated research in brain physiology has shown that specific localization of function does exist. Lashley had been studying only one type of learning behavior in only one type of animal, and his instruments were crude by modern standards. With better instruments, different animals, and more complex learning tasks, brain researchers showed that damaging the brain in particular locations did in fact have different effects on learning behavior. Clinical neurologists had long since observed similar differences in patients who suffered localized brain injuries. In 1964, an influential psychologist-pediatrician, Herbert Birch, published a collection of research and clinical papers supporting the modern neurological position: "Brain damage may vary with respect to etiology, extent, type of lesion, locus, duration of damage, rate at which the damage has been sustained, time of life, and developmental stage at which the injury has occurred."[5] The behavior resulting from these variances might be quite different. Birch was not telling us to drop the concept of brain injury, only to become more knowledgeable about what it really meant.

WERNER'S CONTRIBUTION

Besides Lashley, another theorist had an important influence on Strauss. This was Heinz Werner, a Gestalt psychologist who, like Strauss, was a refugee from Nazi Germany. Werner shared with other Gestalt theorists a conviction that learning and development produced a restructuring of the mind. Werner was particularly interested in the process of differentiation, a term borrowed from biology that referred to such embryological phenomena as the budding of fingers from the stub of a hand. Once differentiation was complete, a functional integration had to take place—through practice, the fingers had to become able to work together. The complementary processes of differentiation and integration characterized many forms of biological growth, and Werner believed them to characterize mental growth as well. Note how compatible this notion is with that of brain equipotentiality. In effect, Werner thought mental development began with an equipotentiality of the mind. Gradually, specific capacities differentiated out of the mental mass. Once formed, the capacities had to be integrated. As presented in his remarkable book *The Comparative Psychology of Mental Development,* Werner believed he saw these principles in many forms of development—in animals, children, primitive humans, and psychopathological persons.[6]

For example, Werner believed that the development of number concepts began with the "natural number space" of the hand. He noted similarities between children who counted on their fingers and primitive people who counted on theirs, and also found it significant that finger agnosia (inability to tell, with your eyes closed, which finger was tapped) was associated with arithmetic disabilities. The next step in the differentiation of the number schema was "dominantly optical in nature." Werner was not sure how this transition occurred, but cited such examples as "children will frequently pick up the objects they are counting and still later only point to them; finally only a glance is necessary." This glance presumably indicates that important mental developments are taking place. "Only those pupils who have developed . . . methods for dealing with optical numerical forms are able to deal with abstract number concepts."[7]

On the basis of such theorizing and experimentation, Werner and his colleagues developed curricula. A good example can be found in "Principles and Methods of Teaching Arithmetic to Mentally Retarded Children" by

Doris Carrison (a teacher) and Werner, published in 1943.[8] The program incorporated Werner's views that development normally moved from tactile-kinesthetic forms of expression and representation, through the visual, to the abstract. Applications to arithmetic learning were straightforward. Children first worked with large materials which actively involved their whole bodies. They were then transferred to smaller devices (such as pegboards) which reduced motor involvement but did not eliminate it. Always the materials presented salient visual patterns. Eventually the numerical ideas would lose their dependency upon spatial, concrete properties and emerge as true abstractions.

Werner's interest in perception had a strong influence on Strauss, and subsequently on the field of learning disabilities. The quality of Werner's theorizing is illustrated by his 1944 article "Development of Visuo-Motor Performance on the Marble-Board Test in Mentally Retarded Children."[9] The marble boards were eleven-inch squares, each containing ten rows of ten holes each. Two boards were used. The experimenter (out of the child's sight) made a pattern of red and black marbles on one board. The pattern was then shown to the child, who copied it on his own board. The experimenter used a scoring system which noted the sequence of the child's moves as well as his accuracy. The particular patterns are shown in Figure 1.

On the basis of the sequential data, Werner carried out a higher-order analysis of what he called "configurational organization." As could be predicted from his general developmental theory, Werner looked for an integration of clearly articulated (differentiated) parts. "The child copies, for instance, Pattern 2 by building first one square, then the other. Such performance presupposes obviously that the child recognized the two subforms with respect to each other and to the whole."

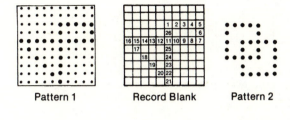

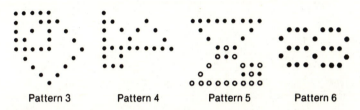

Figure 1. Six patterns of the marble-board test and a sample record.

Deficient performances were characterized by too much attention to the whole or by too much attention to the parts. Both of these conditions indicated a less mature level of activity. Still more primitive was a strictly linear performance, where the child was guided by lines and apparently did not perceive the form-characteristics of the patterns at all. The four types of configurational organization are shown in Figure 2.

THE STRAUSS SYNDROME

The hyperactivity and distractibility of brain-injured children were of great concern to Strauss. In their paper on disorders of conceptual thinking, Strauss and Werner summarized the general behaviors which they believed to characterize brain-injured children.[10]

1. *Forced responsiveness to stimuli.* Any noise, movement, or object immediately captured the child's atten-

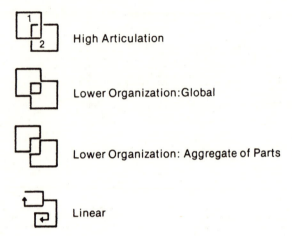

Figure 2. Types of configurational organization in construction of Pattern 2.

tion. Goldstein earlier had seen similar behaviors in brain-damaged adults, and called the phenomenon "stimulus bonding." The term reflected his observation that a passing stimulus seemed to compel the patient's attention. This was quite different from distractibility motivated by boredom.

2. *Pathological fixation.* Brain-injured children were thought to be perseverative in nature. Once they began a simple task like bead stringing, for example, they continued it much longer than a normal child would. That seemed to contradict the distractibility characteristic, but it may have been part of the same system. The child perseverated because the stimulus continued to capture his attention. Probably it continued to seem new to him.

3. *Disinhibition.* Excessive motor activity resulted in the type of behavior we now refer to as hyperactivity. Strauss thought that brain-damaged children were especially attentive to stimulus features that elicited motor activities.

The "bounciness" of a round object, for example, might be especially salient to the child. (I once knew a child who could never be trusted with pencils. The "jabbiness" of a sharp pencil point was more than he could resist.)

4. *Dissociation.* This referred to Werner's concept of integration. The brain-injured child was believed unable to comprehend a pattern as a whole. Instead, he would aggregate parts, as shown in Figure 2. The integration failure manifested itself in a variety of activities. Generally, the child was disorganized in almost everything he did.

These characteristics led Strauss and Lehtinen to design a learning environment for brain-injured children which was quite different from a traditional classroom. The special environment decreased the stimulation of the child. Walls were left plain, windows were covered, even the child's study materials were cut out of the distracting context of illustrated workbooks and mounted on plain paper. Often the child worked in a screened area that insulated him from the sight and sound of others.[11]

HINSHELWOOD'S CONTRIBUTION

Reading difficulties are far and away the most frequent component of any learning-disability syndrome. If we can understand what the reading disorders are all about, we will have solved a large proportion of the learning-disability puzzle.

In 1968, dyslexia was defined as follows by the Interdisciplinary Committee on Reading Problems: "A disorder of children, who despite conventional classroom experience, fail to attain the language skills of reading, writing, and spelling commensurate with their intellectual abilities."[12] What definitions preceded this one?

Early medical theory centered on the work of James

Hinshelwood, a Scottish ophthalmologist with an interest in neurology. James Hinshelwood began publishing in 1895 on a mysterious affliction known as acquired word-blindness, a sudden loss of the ability to read. His summary monograph, *Congenital Word-Blindness,* was published in 1917.[13] Hinshelwood had an explicit theory of the role of the brain in reading, and he tested it clinically. His theory was that there must be separate places in the brain for visual memory of the general everyday type, and visual word memory. If that were true, Hinshelwood said, then it should be possible to find pure cases of each. He set about collecting cases from his own practice and through contact with other physicians.

Everyday visual memory. In 1896, Hinshelwood published a report of a tailor who was fired from his job because he had lost the ability to perform it.[14] Hinshelwood noted that many important aspects of visual memory are represented by tailoring skills. One must have a memory for shapes (patterns) and for how they fit together. "Even in simple stitching the visual memory comes into play and guides the complicated movements of hand and fingers." One must also remember where one's spools and scissors are kept. The tailor's fellow workers were especially annoyed by the fact that he kept forgetting where he had put things and spent more time looking for them than sewing. The poor tailor also began to forget his way home.

But he could *perceive* things normally. Thus, Hinshelwood wrote, we must distinguish between a visual perceptual center and a visual memory center. "The accumulated riches of our life experiences . . . are stored up in a special cerebral area, the visual memory center . . . Derangements of this center are evidenced by the various forms of mind-blindness. The objects are distinctly seen, but they convey no information to the individual since they are no longer recognized by him," that is, they can no longer activate memories.[15]

Hinshelwood diagnosed the tailor as having localized brain damage brought on by alcoholism. He thought the locale was in the vicinity of the *angular gyri*. The exact location is not important at the moment; the point is that Hinshelwood believed the visual memory center of the everyday type to have been affected. True, the patient had also lost the ability to read, thus proving, Hinshelwood said, that word memory was a subsystem of general visual memory without being identical to it. Word-blindness is usually defined only in cases where general visual memory remains intact. Theoretically it must exist in the broader instance as well, and Hinshelwood offered his tailor as proof.

Visual word-memory. The most common types of dyslexia are characterized by an inability to recognize words. Individual letters or numbers may be recognized quite well—and, more important, groups of numbers (1062 read as "one thousand and sixty-two"). Hinshelwood thought such facts indicated that there must be separate (but adjacent) memory centers for words, letters, and numbers. To prove this, he needed cases of pure word-blindness, and they came readily to hand. One of Hinshelwood's reports in 1898 concerned a man of fifty-three who lost the ability to read words after having a stroke. He could read letters, numbers, and groups of numbers fluently. He could also write to dictation and copy words correctly, but could not read what he had written. On the basis of this one symptom, Hinshelwood recognized that the man must have had a stroke. "I gave it as my opinion that the inability to read was not due to any ocular defect, but to a lesion in the visual word-memory centre situated in the *angular* and *supra-marginal gyri* on the left side of the brain and supplied by a branch of the Sylvian artery, that the lesion was a small hemorrhage or more probably thrombosis occluding that branch of the Sylvian artery supplying the centre."[16] Hinshelwood predicted that additional symptoms of stroke would appear, and they did. The patient developed paralysis and aphasia, and died about nine weeks later.

It was during this period that an important scientific notion appeared in the medical literature: dyslexia might be present in some people from birth. Congenital dyslexia, if it existed, should produce many of the same symptoms as those produced by brain injury in adults.

A school doctor by the name of James Kerr was awarded a prize by the Royal Statistical Society in 1896 for an essay on school hygiene which included reference to word-blindness in children.[17] But Hinshelwood preferred to attribute the discovery to a physician named Pringle Morgan. Pringle Morgan said that, in a paper by Hinshelwood published in 1895, he could find no reference to the possibility that the condition described by Hinshelwood might also be congenital.[18] So Pringle Morgan sent in a note to the *British Medical Journal* on November 7, 1896, describing a fourteen-year-old boy who might be an instance of congenital word-blindness.[19] Hinshelwood promptly wrote a letter to the editor commending the good doctor, advising him to encourage the boy to keep working and drawing parallels between Pringle Morgan's boy and his own (adult) cases.[20]

Although Pringle Morgan (or Kerr) must be credited for the initial insight, Hinshelwood went on to do the scholarly work. Hinshelwood's book *Congenital Word-Blindness* has become a classic. Here is a case from it.

A boy, 12 years of age, was brought in March 1902 to the Glasgow Eye Infirmary by his mother, to see if there was anything wrong with his eyesight. The boy had been seven years at school, and there had been from the outset the greatest difficulty in teaching him to read. The boy should have been in Standard V, but was now, after seven years, only in Standard II, and he could not get out of it because of his reading. He had made no complaint whatever about his vision, but his mother had brought him to the Eye Infirmary in order to discover if his eyesight had anything to do with his difficulty. His mother stated that he was in every other respect a sharp and intelligent boy. He had no difficulty with arithmetic, and could keep up with the other scholars easily in this department. He was now working at compound addition. His mother said that the other boys laughed at him in class, and that when he became excited his reading was worse than ever. He concealed his defect for a time by learning his lesson by heart, so that when it came to be his turn and he got a few words at the beginning, he could repeat the lesson by heart. His auditory memory, therefore, was evidently very good. On examining him I found that his reading was very defective for a boy who had been seven years at school. He could rarely read by sight more than two or three words, but came to a standstill every second or third word, and was unable to proceed unless he were allowed to spell out the word aloud, thus appealing to his auditory memory, or to spell it silently with his lips, thus appealing to his memory of speech movements . . . The words he stuck at were chiefly polysyllables, but this was not always the case, as he often failed to recognise by sight even simple monosyllabic words. He spelt very well, and when asked to spell the words which he had failed to recognise by sight, he nearly always did so without any difficulty. He read all combinations of figures with the greatest fluency up to millions. I made him do several sums up to compound addition. All of these he did smartly and correctly. His mother informed me that he had a splendid memory and could learn things by heart very easily. I wrote to his schoolmaster for information about the boy. He replied that the lad had experienced throughout his whole career in the school the greatest difficulty in learning to read, which had kept him very much behind in his progress through the school. He was strong in arithmetic, good at spelling, and average in other subjects, including geography and history.

"I have never," said his master, "seen a case similar to this one in my twenty-five years' experience as a teacher. There is another boy in his class who is quite as poor a reader, but this other boy is all-round poor, showing no sign of smartness in anything."[21]

I have quoted this at length because it remains one of the best descriptions around of dyslexic behavior. The syndrome has certainly not changed since the turn of the century, and neither have our informal methods of diagnosing and defining it.

ORTON'S CONTRIBUTION

In 1925 a paper appeared in the *Archives of Neurology and Psychiatry* entitled "Word-Blindness in School Children." The author was a physician who specialized in neurology, Samuel T. Orton, and the paper presented his new theory of dyslexia—one based on the notion of hemispheric imbalance.[22] In Figure 3, we see an example taken from his 1937 book, *Reading, Writing, and Speech Problems in Children*.[23] Orton believed that written productions were something like a printout of information stored in the brain. Mirror writing therefore showed that the information must be stored in more than one orientation. It had been known for some time that the left hemisphere was responsible for the storage and produc-

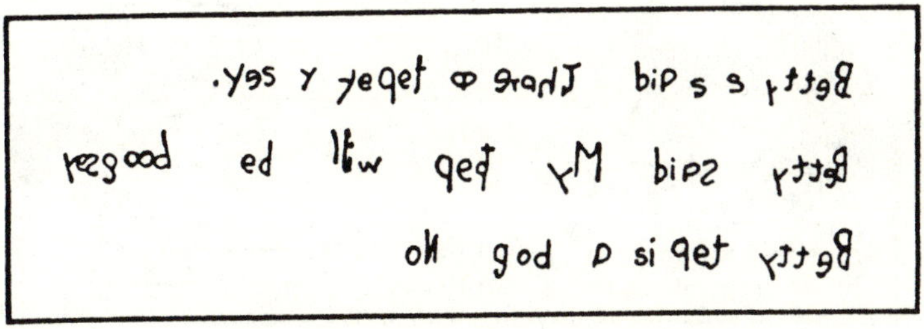

Figure 3. Mirror writing by a left-handed boy.

tion of language. Less was known about the functions of the right hemisphere, but Orton believed that they reflected the activities of the left. "The exact symmetrical relationship of the two hemispheres," he wrote in 1925, "would lead us to believe that the groups of cells irradiated by any visual stimulus in the right hemisphere are the exact mirrored counterpart of those in the left." Further, these mirrored images were remembered. The right hemisphere contained a mnemonic record, a reflected duplicate of information in the left hemisphere. These records could trigger matching motor activity. "The tendency common in young children to mirrored or reversed writing . . . points to the existence in the brain of a mnemonic record in mirrored form which serves as a pattern for these motor expressions."[24]

Learning to read and write correctly, then, was a matter of learning which hemispheric image to pay attention to. Normally a child learned that the left hemispheric renditions were the correct ones. In some cases, however, this learning did not develop normally. Figure 4, from Orton's 1925 paper, schematizes the distribution of certain types of cortical cells. The first, "visual perceptive," were the initial receivers of sensory information. Orton called that cortical level the "arrival platform." The next level up, "visual recognitive," contained brain cells that

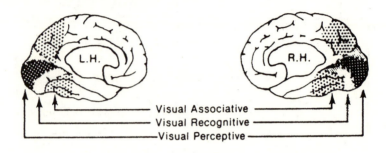

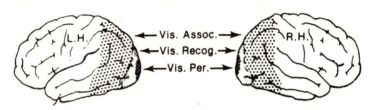

Figure 4. Distribution of three types of cortical tissue.

facilitated visual association of a limited type. Object recognition occurred at this level, but object *meaning* could occur only at the next level: "visual associative." In this area of the brain, connections could be made with other information from sensory and motor areas.

Orton believed that either hemisphere could effectively perform perceptive and recognitive activities, but that associative activities had to be performed by the left hemisphere alone. His evidence for that belief was straightforward, neurologically. Brain injury at the first and second levels did not impair behavior unless it occurred in both hemispheres. Simple perception and recognition could apparently be managed by whichever hemisphere remained intact. But third-level injury was a different story: damage to the right hemisphere made no difference, but damage to the left hemisphere produced word-blindness. To Orton, this suggested that "the process of learning to read entails the elision from the focus of attention" of the right hemispheric images. When the left hemisphere was unable to perform that critical suppressive function, confusions and delays would result. There would be distortions of the motor output in both speech and writing, interference in the linking of visual symbols and sounds, and subsequent failure to associate sounds and meaning. Orton called the whole disaster "strephosymbolia." The Greek roots of the term—*strepho* and *symbolon*—mean "twisted" and "signs."

Orton described five clusters of disabled behavior which he believed to represent dominance failure of the left hemisphere.[25]

1. *Developmental dyslexia*: unusual difficulty in learning to read, but no evidence of accompanying physical, mental, or emotional abnormality. There was normal auditory development and often a display of good intelligence and imagination in solving the problem of not being able to read. For example, the child might become very proficient at guessing the meaning of words and passages. Vision and visual-motor coordination skill in games like basketball were normal and often superior. As Orton pointed out, if you could not read road signs, you had to develop other ways of finding your way home. The reading disability took the form of letter confusion, letter reversals, word confusions and reversals, severe spelling difficulties, and often difficulties in writing.

2. *Developmental dysgraphia*: special difficulty in learning to write. This might accompany reading disability or exist by itself. Sometimes it took the form of extreme slowness in forming letters. In other cases, illegibility was the problem. Writing might be improved by a shift

to the opposite hand or by a shift in direction—some dysgraphic children could do mirror writing as well (or as poorly) as normal writing, or they could write with either hand. They might also be able to write better if they did not watch their hands.

3. *Developmental word-deafness (receptive aphasia)*: difficulty in recognizing the spoken word, delay and distortion of speech, but normal hearing. The child could understand environmental sounds quite well—car horns or barking dogs—but showed confusion in understanding words. Such a child might show a lack of attention to words because the words carried little meaning. The word-deaf child in effect disregarded words, whereas normal children disregarded meaningless environmental sounds. Because aural understanding was such an important component of intelligence, word-deaf children might appear retarded. Functionally, of course, they were, but their retardation resulted from a specific disability in processing language. Speech in these children was usually slow to develop. Verbal output showed distortion and confusion that reflected mishearings. For example, the child might say "pose" for "suppose," or "repeller" for "propeller," or "atween" for "between." Syntactical disorders might be present: the child might say "I have spoking." Generally, such children also developed reading and writing disorders.

4. *Developmental expressive aphasia*: slow development and disorder of speech, but good understanding of the spoken word (that is, no word-deafness). These children did not show an inattention to spoken language and usually tried very hard to express themselves. They recognized errors in their own speech and in the speech of others. Sometimes there was a speech defect, such as a lisp or a stutter. Once speech began to develop, it usually proceeded swiftly.

5. *Developmental dyspraxia*: abnormal clumsiness similar to the type of clumsiness exhibited by a right-handed person attempting to use his left hand. A dyspraxic child seemed to have "two left hands and two left feet," almost literally. There might be a delay in learning to walk, run, button clothes, tie shoes, handle spoons, skip, jump rope, ride tricycles. Speech muscles and small hand muscles might also be affected. Hence, the dyspraxic child might also show speech and writing disorders.

Orton believed that all of these disorders resulted from confusions and conflicts at the associative level. The conflict was quite literally between the left and the right hemisphere. Normally no conflict developed because the left hemisphere controlled the operations of speech, writing, and reading. In the syndromes Orton described, however, the left hemisphere was not in control.

FOUNDING THE FUTURE

The founding fathers of the field now called learning disabilities were remarkably astute. The diagnostic and research guidelines they began to lay down almost one hundred years ago can still be detected in contemporary theory, research, and practice. They didn't know exactly what the problems were, and neither do we. But, as it turned out, we are still working in the ballparks that Strauss, Werner, Hinshelwood, and Orton mapped out.

Some children have difficulties mastering specific school tasks—difficulties which do not resemble those of retarded children, but which do resemble the difficulties of people who have suffered strokes and other brain injuries. The early concepts that guide us are clothed today in different terminology and paradigms, such as the information processing paradigm, but they are all still there.

J. Lee Wiederholt, who published a short history of learning disabilities in 1974, and who is now the editor of the *Journal of Learning Disabilities,* refers to the period reviewed in this chapter as the foundations phase of the field.[26] We turn next to what Wiederholt calls the transition phase. This was characterized by the entry of many new groups into the field—educators, psychologists, parents, and policy makers—who, to some extent, wrested the field away from its medical foundations.

Losing touch with one's roots can create problems, as we will see.

3/ The Transitional Period

The official onset of the field called learning disabilities was a talk given by Samuel A. Kirk, then of the University of Illinois, on April 6, 1963.[1] Kirk was addressing a conference sponsored by the Fund for Perceptually Handicapped Children. The conference leaders had asked Kirk to suggest an alternative term for the children in question. Terms then in use, in addition to "perceptually handicapped," included "minimally brain-damaged" and "exogenous."

Kirk reviewed a number of terms, pointing out that because some of them referred to brain processes which could not be examined directly, there was no way of knowing if the terms were accurate. Further, some of the terms did not indicate a domain of treatment, as diagnostic terms should. If a child is diagnosed as diabetic, for example, his treatment is indicated. What treatment does the term "minimally brain-damaged" indicate? "Reading handicap," on the other hand, carries remedial information, although the term might not be sufficiently general. A good categorical term, Kirk said, would not only be general, it would also demarcate appropriate assessment, training, and management procedures. He went on:

Recently, I have used the term "learning disabilities" to describe a group of children who have disorders in development in language, speech, reading, and associated communication skills needed for social interaction. In this group I do not include children who have sensory handicaps such as blindness or deafness, because we have methods of managing and training the deaf and the blind. I also exclude from this group children who have generalized mental retardation.[2]

That struck exactly the right chord. Following a period of discussion, the conference voted to call itself the Association for Children with Learning Disabilities (this was later modified to include adults, and has been most recently renamed Learning Disabilities Association of America). Over a decade later, P.L. 94-142 incorporated much of Kirk's original language.

Several chords of ensuing disharmony were also struck at that 1963 meeting, however. They arose from the fact that Kirk had not spelled out what some of his professional colleagues considered to be the scientific ancestry of his position—specifically, the work of Strauss and Werner.[3] Their work at the Wayne County Training School had dealt entirely with moderately to severely handicapped children, most of whom were retarded. The research question had been: Can we distinguish between the retardation that arises from inheritance and the retardation that arises from brain injury? Strauss and Werner believed that the two types of retardation could be distinguished in the behavior of the children. They had labeled the inherited type of retardation "endogenous" and the brain-injured type "exogenous." It was the exogenous group of children who were, in the minds of some of Kirk's professional colleagues, to be henceforth renamed learning-disabled.

But Kirk did not spell this out in so many words, and

two kinds of confusions followed. First, Kirk's remarks about the inappropriateness of brain-damage labels were interpreted to mean that brain damage itself should not be considered a factor in learning disabilities. Second, his remarks about the exclusion of retardation were interpreted to mean that retardation should not be considered a factor either. He was understood as saying that children henceforth to be called learning-disabled were neither brain-damaged nor retarded.

To parents and to many professionals this was joyful news. It meant that what had previously looked like brain damage or retardation was really nothing of the kind. Instead, it was a learning disability, a new type of disorder that did not carry connotations of retardation or brain damage.

This was probably not what Kirk meant. He had no scientific basis for postulating a brand new type of learning disorder—one which was not caused by either familial retardation or by nonfamilial brain damage. As he clarified in 1971, his major focus was on the *specificity* of the disorder:

> The word "special" or "specific" is very important in this definition [of learning disabilities] since it indicates that the child has a definite retardation in one or more areas but that this retardation is not caused by a sensory deficit or severe mental retardation, and that it exists in spite of the fact that the child has certain abilities in other areas. It also indicates that the child's [specific] retardation is not due to lack of educational experiences.[4]

Nevertheless, the belief persisted that retardation and/or brain damage was not a factor in learning disabilities. The specificity that Kirk described was differently interpreted.

PROCESS TRAINING APPROACHES

Since the middle of the last century, there have been many versions of the belief that minds, like bodies, are composed of components that have unique functions. In phrenology, for example, love, signified by one bump on the skull, was different in both location and function from memory, signified by another bump. Even earlier, Augustine and Thomas Aquinas had advanced theories of what came to be called faculty psychology, which described faculties such as memory, will, and inventiveness. Toward the end of the last century, the English biologist Francis Galton pioneered the idea of precisely measuring these traits (as they had come to be called). That effort led to the modern fields of psychometrics and individual differences. Those fields follow strict, mathematically based rules for defining and measuring individual traits.[5]

Most early specialists in learning disabilities adopted the general idea that composites of traits or faculties—which they called processes—were activated when a child performed a task. Weakness in one or more of the processes would account for the child's failure on the task. Improving the child's performance was therefore a straightforward matter of strengthening that particular process, rather like strengthening arm muscles to improve a child's batting average.

Although some of these specialists (Samuel Kirk, for example) adopted the rigorous psychometric rules of the period, many others did not. They created test-like instruments, but they used them informally. They made inferences about what was wrong with a child's processing primarily on the basis of their own intuitions and experience. Their justification for that approach was practical (though circular): if the remedies they prescribed were successful, that proved their initial diagnosis to be correct.

I will describe briefly the work of four early process theorists: Jean Ayres, who focused on sensory integration; Newell Kephart, on perceptual-motor matching; Marianne Frostig, on visual-perceptual training; and Samuel Kirk's own work on psychological features of communication.

JEAN AYRES: SENSORIMOTOR INTEGRATION

The cornerstone of Ayres's work was her belief that learning disabilities resulted from underlying deviations in neural functioning which had developmental roots: something had gone wrong with the normal course of neurological development. Treatment, therefore, was intended to enhance normal maturation. If development could be put back on track, the child's neurological disorganization would be corrected, and improvements in thinking and learning would follow.[6]

Ayres was initially trained as an occupational therapist, and her tests and programs may still be observed in some rehabilitation clinics. Ayres produced an elaborate (but scientifically incorrect) theory of brain function and development. For example, she believed that sensory and subcortical systems (such as balancing mechanisms) were the foundations of higher-order processes (such as learning and problem solving). Learning disabilities, she said, arose from deficiencies in sensory and subcortical systems, and could be treated accordingly.

Three general types of dysfunction were at the root of learning disabilities, Ayres believed: (a) deficient intermodality associations (poor sight-sound coordination, for example); (b) inadequate inhibition of motor or sensory impulses; and (c) insufficient feedback regulation (eye-hand guidance, for example). Ayres developed methods for assessing disorders of form and space perception, of the capacity for planning and executing motor actions, of posture and balance, and of sensory and language functions. The first version of her test was called the Southern California Sensory Integration Test. A newer version, published in 1989, is called the Sensory Integration and Praxis Test. (The term "praxis" refers to motor organization and control.)

In Ayres therapy, the general principle is that a particular type of sensory stimulation, in eliciting a particular type of response, will enhance brain organization, which will in turn improve learning and thinking. For example, a child may be spun in a hammock or rotating chair. Ayres thought that many learning-disabled children failed to display normal dizzy responses. The appearance of dizziness, Ayres believed, showed that "dormant pathways" were becoming active; the activation of these pathways would promote broad forms of sensory integration, which would in turn enhance academic skills.

Therapy programs also included postural exercises, balancing exercises, tactile stimulation with cloths, brushes, and lotions, crawling on hands and knees, muscle contractions, scooter-board activities, and being rolled in a cloth-lined barrel.

NEWELL KEPHART: PERCEPTUAL-MOTOR MATCHING

Newell Kephart worked with Werner and Strauss at the Wayne County Training School for a few years, and published with them. Following Werner, Kephart believed that tasks, such as drawing a square, could be broken down into basic skills—visualizing the square, guiding the pencil, and so on—which should then be taught separately. Kephart had an elaborate theory of development, derived in part from his association with Werner. He developed a Perceptual Motor Rating Scale to assess phases of development that were weak and needed training. These included sensorimotor phases, ocular control, and form perception.[7]

Children who needed sensorimotor strengthening were given exercises on walking boards, balance beams, and trampolines, and engaged in stunts and games such as elephant walking. Ocular control training included following balls or lights with the eyes and following moving objects with a finger as well as with the eyes. Form perception training involved matching patterns with puzzles, pegboards, and stick figures.

A fundamental tenet of Kephart's was what he called "the perceptual-motor match."[8] Figure 5 illustrates Kephart's point. Sensory input must be matched to the child's motor awareness of the stimulating materials. This necessitates an internal matching process which involves past experience. Kephart's training programs were all designed to develop that internal stabilization and efficiency.

MARIANNE FROSTIG: VISUAL-PERCEPTUAL TRAINING

Marianne Frostig's work focused on visual-perceptual skills, which she believed to be fundamental to academic

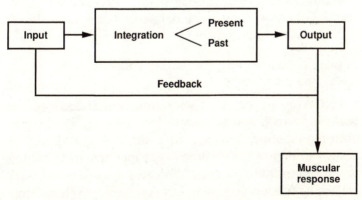

Figure 5. Kephart's perceptual matching routine.

success. She thought that most learning occurred through visual channels, and that learning disabilities could usually be attributed to impaired perceptual development during early childhood.[9] Frostig designed a Developmental Test of Visual Perception. It included subtests of eye-motor coordination, figure-ground detection, form constancy, and spatial constancy.

Remedial training was specific to the subtests. For example, children practiced eye-motor control by coloring and tracing on worksheets. They learned to attend to figure-ground distinctions by practicing on materials like those shown in Figure 6. Note how the series of exercises moves from geometrical forms into academic materials. Perceptual constancy was also practiced first on geometric forms, and then on written words, as shown in Figure 7. The child learned to recognize the same forms in different sizes and orientations, and the same words in different handwritings.

Spatial constancy was invoked by having children follow directions to crawl under, over, and around pieces of furniture. The children thus formulated concepts of spatial stability, despite differences in viewpoints.

Frostig's programs were very popular during the 1960s and 1970s, in part because they were so well structured. Diagnostic and remedial procedures were clearly linked, easy to implement, and interesting to children.

SAMUEL KIRK: PSYCHOLOGICAL FEATURES OF COMMUNICATION

Following up on his own recommendations, Samuel Kirk developed a new system for defining, identifying, and remediating learning disabilities.[10] His model is shown in Figure 8. Psychological functions are activated when one individual communicates with another. Kirk called the functions depicted in Figure 8 "psycholinguistic abilities."

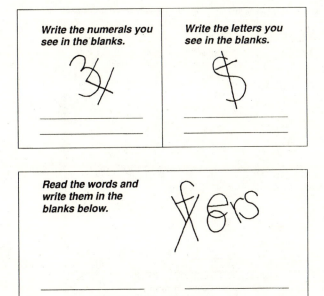

Figure 6. Frostig's figure-ground practice materials.

The model has three dimensions—routes, in effect—through which communications flow. The dimension shown along the left vertical goes from automatic, or meaningless, to representational, or meaningful (2 levels). The dimension along the top horizontal goes from reception to organization to expression (3 levels). The

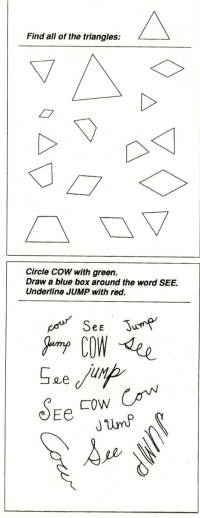

Figure 7. Frostig's form-constancy practice materials.

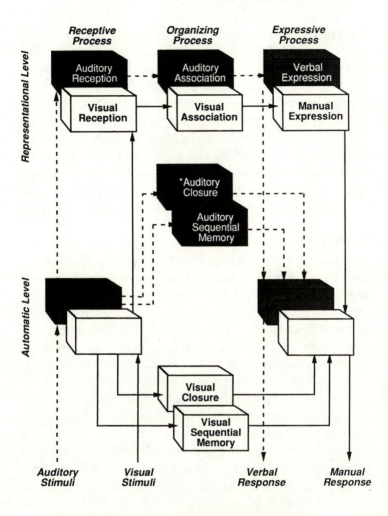

Figure 8. Kirk's model of psycholinguistic processes.

dimension running from back to front goes from auditory to visual (2 levels). The labeled boxes refer to subtests in the Illinois Test of Psycholinguistic Abilities (ITPA). Each test is located at an intersection of the three dimensions. Thus, the Auditory Reception test measures the reception of meaningful material through hearing. The Visual Sequential Memory test measures the ability to organize meaningless visual material. The Visual Association test measures the ability to organize meaningful visual material. Where the boxes are blank, no tests were developed, primarily because they would have had limited diagnostic value.

A child's scores on the ITPA subtests are plotted on a graph to form a profile. The averaged profiles of two groups of children, disabled and nondisabled readers, are shown in Figure 9. It is clear that the main differences between the two groups occur at the automatic level. Let's examine two of these automatic-level subtests: Visual Sequential Memory, which picked up differences between disabled and nondisabled readers, and Auditory Sequential Memory, which did not.

The visual task uses sets of small white tiles with nonsense figures inscribed on them. The child is first shown a picture of two tiles arranged in a line. The picture is displayed for five seconds and then removed. Selecting from his set of tiles, the child must then reproduce the picture. With each trial, more tiles are pictured, and the child's score is derived from the longest sequence of tiles he can reproduce from memory correctly.

The auditory task uses random numbers. The examiner speaks the numbers at a fixed rate, and the child must repeat them back. Again, the child's score is determined from the longest string of random numbers that the child can repeat back correctly.

Both tasks are at the automatic level (the materials are meaningless), both require the child to maintain the se-

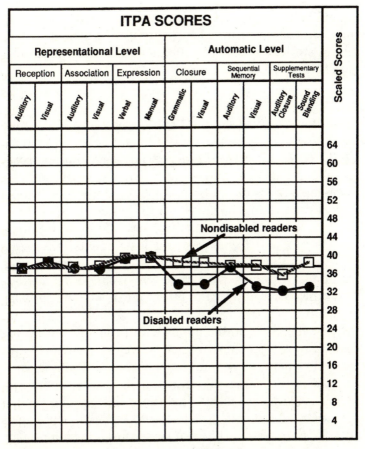

Figure 9. Profiles of ITPA scores for disabled and nondisabled readers.

quential organization of the materials, and each emphasizes a particular modality.

If a child tests low on the visual task, remedial training might include connecting numbered dots to form pictures, putting together a face from scrambled vertical or horizontal strips, or reproducing sequences of letters. If a child tests low on the auditory task, remedial training might include repeating words, repeating sentences, retelling stories, or using sequential words like "before," "after," and "next to."

THE DEMISE OF PROCESS TRAINING

During the 1970s and 1980s, process training approaches were widely evaluated. Were they effective? Could their advocates justify removing children from regular classwork in order to provide them with nonacademic exercises designed to repair underlying psychological processes? The answer from hundreds of evaluation studies was a resounding no.[11] Process training approaches, and the assessment instruments that went along with them, are now very much out of favor, and are almost never seen in public school special education programs. They do continue to appear in some private programs.

I will shortly examine the general problems with process training approaches. First, however, this is a good place to mention several quasi-medical training approaches to learning disabilities that verge on outright quackery. These are often advertised through the popular media, and may lure parents into the hope of a magic cure for their child. Although these programs may seem similar to the programs described above, they are not direct descendants of them.

"MAGIC CURES" FOR LEARNING DISABILITIES

Doman-Delacato patterning. This system is based on a wildly erroneous theory of brain development and organization.[12] Children with learning problems (including severely defective children) are treated by moving them through a series of exercises designed to reconstitute what Glen Doman and Carl Delacato believed to be phases of brain development. Thus, the child practices crawling (or, in the case of a child who cannot move for himself, his arms and legs are moved in a crawling pattern by a team of adults), then creeping, and so on. These exercises, according to Doman and Delacato, recapitulate the order of brain development in the infant in order to stimulate new brain growth in the older child. Learning disabilities that were the result of damage to certain brain cells can thus be overcome, according to Doman and Delacato. Alternative brain cells will be stimulated to grow in their place. Other treatments include breathing one's own carbon dioxide exhalations in a plastic bag.

The following organizations, among others, have issued statements of caution regarding the Doman-Delacato claims: The American Academy for Cerebral Palsy, the Canadian Association for Retarded Children, and the American Academy of Pediatrics, which noted "that the patterning treatment offers no special merit, that the claims of its advocates are unproven, and that the demands on families are so great that in some cases there may be harm in its use."[13]

The Levinson theory of vestibular dysfunction. Harold Levinson has proposed a theory that reading disabilities are caused by dysfunctions in the vestibular system.[14] This is the system that controls balance. Disturbances in this system can lead to dizziness and seasickness. After diagnosing a child as having defects in the vestibular system, Levinson prescribes anti–motion sickness medication. He believes that such medication will ameliorate if not cure dyslexia.

There is no reliable medical evidence that learning-disabled children in general, or dyslexic children in particular, have vestibular ailments.[15] It is true that people with such ailments may have difficulty reading. (Have you ever tried to read during a bout of motion sickness?) But there is no scientific support for a claim that reading or learning difficulties could therefore originate in disorders of the vestibular system.

Optometric visual training. Optometrists have long advertised themselves as specialists in reading problems.[16] Their training programs emphasize eye-motor exercises, such as tracking a pendulum. However, dyslexia is not caused by defects in the musculature of eye movements (see Chapter 6). Dyslexia originates in the central nervous system, deep inside the brain. Optometric training programs generally are based on incorrect theories of reading processes and their remediation, and of the role of eye movements in reading.[17]

The following organizations have issued statements cautioning against optometric remedial reading programs: the American Academy of Pediatrics, the American Academy of Ophthalmology and Otolaryngology, the American Association of Ophthalmology, and the American Association for Pediatric Ophthalmology and Strabismus. One statement reads in part: "Learning disability and dyslexia . . . require a multidisciplinary approach from medicine, education, and psychology in diagnosis and treatment. Eye care should never be instituted in isolation when a patient has a reading problem . . . No known scientific evidence supports claims for improving the academic abilities of learning-disabled or dyslexic children with treatment based solely on . . . visual training (muscle exercises, ocular pursuit, glasses.)"[18]

Chiropractic treatment. Chiropractic practice originated in the theories of Daniel David Palmer, a tradesman who operated a "magnetic healing" studio in Iowa in the late nineteenth century. Chiropractors emphasize spinal mechanics, but (where state law permits) may use a variety of additional treatments, such as nutrition, physiotherapy, or diathermy. Some chiropractic clinics are now offering treatment for learning disabilities and dyslexia, usually based on a theory by Carl Ferreri and Richard Wainwright that learning disabilities are caused by misalignment of two cranial bones, the spenoid and the temporal, producing pressure on the brain.[19] Dyslexia is alleged to result from this pressure, and to be cured by realignment of the bones. (Let me note hastily that cranial bones do not move, especially not, as alleged by Ferreri and Wainwright, every time you breathe.)

The following quotation from a reviewer of this system sums up the problems to be found with all "magic cures" for learning disabilities:

> The basis for the theory and treatment is a book [fill in the title of any book offering a magic cure]. Produced by an obscure publisher, and distributed by [the authors'] Neural Organization Technique Centers [fill in the name of any other magic cure center], the book offers no research data aside from a study done by [the author]. This article, cited frequently in the book as the research basis for . . . the [curative] technique, is a one-page description . . . that appeared in a journal unknown in the scientific community, and does not employ standard research practice . . .
>
> The authors use an approach not too dissimilar from those proposed by others who have reported sudden cures for learning disabilities. They report a theory and suggest that it is based on research facts. If one makes the effort to seek out the references cited, it is found that no

such research facts exist. Further, the theory is based on scientific and anatomical beliefs that are counter to established knowledge.[20]

UNDERLYING FALLACIES

Our review of process training approaches and "magic cures" has been quite sparse. Thousands of programs across the nation have claimed to cure or at least substantially ameliorate learning disabilities. Some of them are cases of outright quackery. Some are well-meant but ignorant. Some are honest efforts to reach beyond current theory, based on an intuitive recognition that a better theory must exist, one that hasn't yet been worked out scientifically.

Most of the early process theorists, as represented by Ayres, Kephart, Frostig, and Kirk, fit into the last category. They were attempting to reach beyond the rat-driven learning theories of their time, and some of their work foreshadowed the advent of a new field, called information processing psychology, which was coming into existence in the early 1960s. There will be more about this new field, and the framework it provides for the study of learning disabilities, in Chapter 4.

Most of the "magic cures" (and, it must be admitted, many of the process training approaches) are simply bad science. They are based on incorrect theories of brain function, vision, biochemical functions, anatomy, and so on. Parents can easily avoid these traps by consulting with a bona fide specialist (someone whose credentials are beyond dispute) before signing up a child for some unorthodox course of treatment which claims to have a scientific basis. Ask the specialist if the treatment sounds plausible, safe, and worth the money (which will probably be considerable).

As a general rule of thumb, it is useful to keep in mind that mental processes like perception, auditory sequential memory, and so on, cannot be "strengthened" through some course of treatment. The misconception arises from our habitual ways of thinking about and treating bodily dysfunctions. Weak muscles can be exercised, weak bones can be strengthened with doses of calcium. But the mind just doesn't work like that. The mind isn't made up of separable processes. Perception, for example, can't be separated from other mental processes, the way muscle can be separated from bone. Perception is a portion of a stream of mental activities that changes from task to task. Think of all the different tasks that involve perception: watching the trajectory of a ball, identifying a bird, scanning the road for oncoming cars, searching a line of print for a particular letter, reading, listening for a baby's cry, listening to a teacher call the roll, listening for your own name, listening for the recess bell, feeling in your desk for a book, feeling in your desk for contraband (chewing gum), and on and on. Each such activity sets in motion a unique pattern of neurological activities. The portion of the pattern that will be called perception will differ from task to task. Scientists who study perception therefore precisely specify the tasks they are using, and emphasize that their findings cannot be generalized beyond those particular tasks.

The example of perception could be applied to any mental process: memory, short-term memory, auditory or visual memory, sequencing, word retrieval, attention—all the processes that one thinks of in connection with learning disabilities. These principles always hold: (a) a mental process can never exist alone, like a muscle—it is always some portion of a stream of mental processes; (b) the stream of processes changes from task to task; (c) to study a portion of a stream, a scientist must limit his research to a strictly specified task—that is, to a particular stream of mental processes; (d) the results of that research will apply only to tasks of the same type.

As we will see in forthcoming chapters, research conducted according to those principles is producing important new information. Some of these research programs are reexamining concepts first presented earlier in the history of the field. The best of the old is being preserved within the framework of the new.[21]

4/ Information Processing Research

About a hundred years ago, William James described what he called the "stream of consciousness": "a succession of states, or waves, or fields (or whatever you please to call them), of knowledge, of feeling, of desire, of deliberation, etc., that constantly pass and repass, and that constitute our inner life. The existence of this stream is the primal fact; the nature and origin of it form the essential problem of our science."[1]

At the time, psychologists studied the stream of consciousness introspectively. They reflected upon, characterized, and quantified their own thoughts and sensations. With the advent of behaviorism, this type of research lost favor and disappeared from the scientific scene from about 1915 until the mid-1950s. By then engineers were tracking the flow of information through electronic systems, and a few psychologists had begun to examine the possibility that the flow of information could be similarly tracked through human minds.[2]

A number of ingenious methods were developed. In 1960, for example, George Sperling described a technique for determining how long a brief visual image (a face glimpsed in a flash of lightning, say) persisted in "the mind's eye." The answer: 250 thousandths of a second.[3] In 1964, Saul Sternberg revived a hundred-year-old technique, introduced by a Dutch oculist named Donders, for estimating the number of processing operations that occur between the reception of a stimulus and the output of a response. Suppose you are first given a set of random numbers to hold in mind, and then are asked: "Is the number six in the set?" The speed of your answer will depend upon how many numbers you are holding in mind, how many you have to scan. Sternberg determined that memory scanning occurs at the rate of about 38 milliseconds per item.[4] Other research investigated decision time per se. A negative decision takes about 50 milliseconds longer than an affirmative decision.[5]

By the mid-1970s, when research of this type was beginning to diminish, many processing rates had been determined: how long it takes to generate an image, to search an image (longer to "see" the tail on an elephant, for example, than the tail on a mouse),[6] to retrieve words from memory,[7] to assemble articulatory processes (longer to prepare to utter big words than small ones), to assemble movements (longer to prepare to type a six-letter word than a three-letter word),[8] and so on. Developmental differences were also studied. Processing rates are typically slow in young children, and speed up systematically with growth, in part because of brain maturation and in part because of practice.[9]

Out of this research there grew the general picture of the human information-processing system schematized in Figure 10. The system picks up information from the environment—auditory, visual, and so forth. The receptors detect features of objects (edges, colors, sound frequencies). Psychological and anatomical studies have established that there are areas of the brain, columns of neurons, that are specialized for particular features. A few thousandths of a second after features are detected,

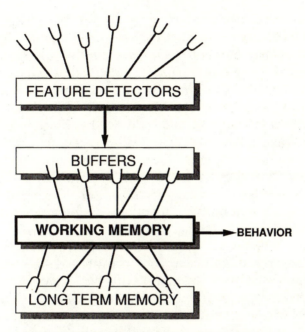

Figure 10. The information processing system.

they are synthesized. This happens so fast that you perceive a whole object, rather than registering edges and colors separately. These mechanisms activate very short-term holding regions of the brain, symbolized as buffers. Sperling was studying the holding region of the visual system.

The central controlling region of the information-processing system is labeled "working memory." This is the executive system. It manages information coming in from the outside, as well as information stored in long-term memory. Working memory has been extensively studied by psychologists. A good deal is known about its capacity, its processing rates, and its self-programming characteristics.[10]

Working memory has a very limited immediate capacity, as illustrated by digit-span studies. Random numbers are recited to a subject at the rate of about one per second. The subject recites them back, first two numbers, then three, and so on. A normal adult won't make any errors until he or she has to recite back about seven numbers. A two-year-old child will be able to recite back only about two; a five-year-old, about four, and so on. As with processing rates, this development is due in part to brain maturation and in part to practice.[11]

Given its limited capacity, how does working memory maintain continuity? Why don't you forget what you're doing from one memory load to the next? Briefly, working memory is activated by goals, which in turn sensitize the system to particular cues, activate regions of knowledge in long-term memory, assemble behavioral output (speech or actions), and respond to feedback.[12] Given the goal of finding out what time it is, you look around for a clock, become sensitive to "clocklike" environmental features, and activate time-telling skills stored in long-term memory. Once the goal is satisfied (by feedback), it drops out of working memory and is replaced by a new goal (finding a place to eat lunch). Your sense of continuity is maintained by these goal-driven programs.

In fact, a number of programs are up and running simultaneously in normal minds. Your program for reading this book may be embedded in a long-term program to understand learning disabilities, which interacts with a nest of programs for teaching. Working memory is a time-sharing system. Attention switches from one program to another. Well-organized minds frequently construct higher-order programs for switching attention efficiently.

Long-term memory has also been studied in detail. It is generally conceptualized as a network of associations.

Remote, sparsely interconnected regions of the network will take longer to activate, as you experience when you try to remember something you didn't learn very well.[13]

APPLICATIONS TO RESEARCH ON LEARNING DISABILITIES

It is possible to imagine a number of ways in which this basic information-processing structure might be disabled. To begin with, there could be defects of the feature-detecting system, short of blindness or deafness, regarding particular features—the black lines of print, or the sounds of speech, for example. As I discuss in Chapter 6, a good case can be made that such problems underlie dyslexia.

What kinds of defects might afflict working memory? Its capacity could be impaired, as indicated by a subnormal digit span. Alternatively, something could be wrong with the way working memory is connected to the buffers or to long-term memory. In that case, critical environmental cues would not be picked up, or available knowledge would not be activated. As still another possibility, there might be defects in attention-switching mechanisms; the ability to alternate between working memory programs could be impaired.

With respect to long-term memory, something could be wrong with the ability to store knowledge of certain types: syntax, or spatial knowledge, for example. If these stores were faulty, then any working memory program that activated them would be faulty. Working memory programs that activated other types of knowledge, such as motor skills, might work fine.

These are only a few ways of thinking about what could go wrong, given a basic information processing structure of the type shown in Figure 10. I will shortly work through a detailed example of how research into information processing problems is conducted. But first I need to explain two important general principles.

PRINCIPLES OF INFORMATION PROCESSING RESEARCH

First, testing of different components of the information processing system must be done with the same task. It is not possible to administer one task to check out the pick-up system, another task to check out working memory, and yet another task to check out long-term memory. It can be very difficult to keep this principle in mind, because we are so accustomed to medical testing procedures, where one test is used to check blood sugar, another test is used to check insulin level, and so on. The information processing system cannot be probed in that way. Every time a task is changed, the entire system operates differently. Hence a single task must be used.

The second general principle is related to the first: If a processing defect appears on one task, it cannot be assumed that the same defect will appear on any other task. This is also difficult to remember. If it is discovered, for example, that learning-disabled children have difficulty retrieving words on a particular word-memorization task, it is very tempting to conclude that learning-disabled children have word-retrieval defects. But this cannot be assumed. The children may not have the slightest bit of difficulty retrieving words during everyday conversation, or shouting directions during a soccer game, or writing a spelling test, or playing Scrabble. Jumping to the conclusion that failure at one task indicates a general defect constitutes what I call the "process transfer fallacy." This was the fallacy at the root of the process training approaches described in Chapter 3. It is extremely important to guard against that fallacy in contemporary information processing research as well.

Keeping those two principles firmly in mind, let us now work through an example of how information processing research is conducted.

LEE SWANSON'S STUDY

Lee Swanson is a professor of psychology at the University of California at Riverside. He has conducted extensive research on the information processing capabilities of learning-disabled children.[14]

In the study described here, Swanson investigated the short-term learning abilities of children who had been classified as slow learners, learning-disabled, average, or gifted.[15] The mean age and verbal IQ of each group are shown in Table 3. Mindful of the problem of misclassification, Swanson constructed the research groups according to strict criteria. Note, for example, that his learning-disabled group matched the average group in IQ, while the slow-learning group did not.

Swanson was looking for evidence that learning defects are localized in working memory. To investigate this, he used a fill-in-the-blank reading task similar to those found in language arts workbooks. Children read sentences that contained a missing noun and selected, from an answer set of two, the noun that filled in the blank most sensibly.

Table 3. Characteristics of Children in Swanson's Study

	Slow learners	Learning-disabled	Average	Gifted
Age	12.7	12.7	12.5	12.4
Verbal IQ	83	104	105	128

The sentences were of two types, and the answer sets were of two types. Half of the sentences were short and simple, and half were elaborated in helpful ways. Half of the answer sets presented an easy choice, and half a hard one.

SENTENCES

Simple: The woman wore a pretty _____.

Elaborative: The woman wore a pretty _____ to the dance.

ANSWER SETS

Easy: dress, foot

Hard: dress, sock

The children were given sentences of all four types in a randomized order. The children were told that the task had two parts. The first part was to fill in the blanks with the word that made the most sense. The second part was to recall the words. They were first to recall the words they had chosen, and then to recall the words they had not chosen. As you can see, the paradigm (called a dual-task paradigm) required the children to perform two tasks simultaneously: complete the sentences, and memorize words.

The efficiency with which you can do several things at once (walk, talk, and eat a sandwich) depends upon how automated the activities are.[16] Because you don't have to think about walking or chewing, you can "put your mind on" conversation. And indeed, you may be surprised to discover that you have finished your sandwich, and arrived at your destination, almost unconsciously. On the other hand, if you are walking over treacherous ice patches, you may forget to eat and lose the thread of your conversation. Your working memory resources are allocated to walking.

This was why Swanson used both easy and hard answer sets. With an easy set, choosing between the two answers would be almost automatic, and working memory resources could be allocated to memorization. With a hard set, choosing would not be automatic, and resources would have to be shared between choosing and memorizing. According to Swanson's hypothesis, sharing working memory resources is exactly what children with learning problems cannot do very well. Therefore the sharpest contrasts among children of different abilities should appear when answer choices were hard.

The results of Swanson's study are shown in Figure 11. All of the groups had roughly the same success recalling words from easy answer sets. With hard answer sets, on the other hand, success varied by groups: slow learners are lowest, learning-disabled are higher, average is still higher, and gifted highest.

Everyone, including the slow learners and the learn-

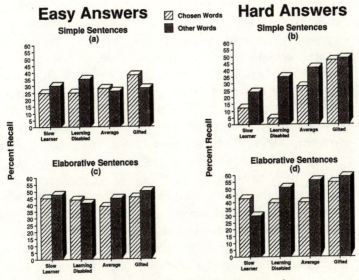

Figure 11. The results of Swanson's research.

ing-disabled, recalled more words from elaborative sentences than from simple ones. That is an important finding, because it has sometimes been argued that a characteristic of slow-learning and learning-disabled children is that they fail to make use of cues provided by verbal elaborations.[17]

The striped bars show the children's recall for the words they chose to fill in the blanks. The shaded bars show their recall for the words they did not choose. Remember that the children knew they were to recall both sets of words. In twelve of the sixteen instances, the shaded bars are higher. The children apparently made a special effort to remember the words they didn't circle.

There is a very large difference between the striped and shaded bars for the learning-disabled group in graph (b). The difference suggests that the effort to remember the unchosen words really took its toll in that group.

Given these results, was Swanson correct in hypothesizing that working memory is the locus of learning problems on tasks of this type? To begin with, there was apparently nothing wrong at the feature detection or buffer level. All the children read the sentences and the answer words aloud, and read them correctly. There was also nothing obviously wrong at the long-term memory level. This can be inferred from the following two results. First, there were no differences among the groups in the correctness of the answers they chose. That shows there were no differences among the groups in knowledge (stored in long-term memory) of word meanings and sentence forms. Everyone recognized that "dress" was right and "foot" was wrong. Everyone also recognized that "sock" was plausible but "dress" was better.

Second, all the children showed improved recall of words from elaborated sentences. Elaborations are effective because they activate long-term memory associations. If the groups were equally helped by elaborations, that means their long-term memory associative capabilities were equivalent.

The locus of the differences between the four groups must therefore be in working memory. Specifically, the groups differed in their ability to handle two tasks simultaneously, if neither task was automated. When it was hard to decide between words, the slow-learning and learning-disabled children had trouble retaining the words. The effort they put into making hard decisions drained resources from memorizing. Additionally, as shown in (b), the effort that learning-disabled children put into making hard decisions, plus the effort they put into remembering unchosen words, drained resources from memorizing chosen words.

Children in the average and gifted groups did not have these "drainage" problems. They efficiently allocated their working memory resources between deciding and memorizing, and carried off both operations successfully. In fact, the recall scores of average and gifted children were even better when they dealt with hard choices. The extra effort they put into choosing apparently helped them to remember. (This is a well-known finding in psychology, sometimes referred to as a "depth of processing" effect.)[18]

IMPLICATIONS FOR REMEDIATION

First of all, we must beware of the process transfer fallacy, and avoid concluding that slow-learning and learning-disabled children have difficulty allocating working memory resources in everything they do. We are talking here only about one particular kind of task, a fill-in-the-blank problem that also has some memorization requirements. This is a fairly common type of task in language arts programs, which is, of course, why Swanson chose to investigate it.

For this particular type of task, the remedial implication is clear: Teach working memory strategies. Teach children with learning problems how to break a complex task into manageable parts, how to monitor their own attention, and how to distribute their study time.[19] Teach them also to recognize when they are confronting a task that may be beyond their capacities. Teach them what to do under those conditions: how to seek counseling, how to request services they need.

I remember a slow-learning twelve-year-old who was participating in an experiment of mine. She appeared with a pencil and paper, and informed me that her teacher had taught her always to make a list of everything she was expected to do. She indeed made such a list of my experimental requirements, and insisted that I discuss and clarify each item. Researchers and teachers will understand my astonishment. I was accustomed to reeling off instructions to children who never questioned them. There now materialized a child who took charge of her learning environment, including me. It was a wonderful object lesson in the academic self-management skills that children can learn if they are fortunate enough to have a teacher who imparts them.

IMPLICATIONS FOR CLASSIFICATION AND PLACEMENT

Swanson's strict control of IQ levels highlights some current issues concerning classification and placement of children with learning problems. His research showed that children in both the slow-learning and the learning-disabled groups had difficulty allocating working memory resources. Does that mean the other differences between them, as represented by their respective IQs, should be dismissed? Should slow-learning and learning-disabled children be educated together? Certainly both groups would benefit from special instruction in working memory strategies on tasks like those Swanson used. Does that mean they should receive such strategy instruction on materials of the same grade level?

Would average and gifted children benefit from strategy instruction, too? If we discover remedial strategies that help learning-impaired children to catch up to non-impaired children, should those strategies be withheld from nonimpaired children? If they are not withheld, does that mean the nonimpaired children will shoot ahead, leaving the learning-impaired children yet again behind?

One indication of Swanson's study is that elaborative materials reduce differences between the children who have learning problems and the children who don't, especially when the task is easy. Graph (c) shows that slow learners recalled as many words from elaborative sentences as the gifted children did. Does that mean all children should be educated in elaboratively rich environments? The answer to that is easy: yes.

The answer to the next question is more difficult: Should all children be given easy tasks, the sort that eliminated differences between slow learners and gifted? If they were, then children of all IQ levels could be educated together, and the slow-learning group would never feel inferior. Is this the political ideal of a democratic educational system? You can see why it is essential to involve social policy experts in learning disabilities research.

My own view is that all these issues are artifacts of an educational system based on outdated principles. If we redesigned public education within the framework of contemporary principles, then the questions raised above would simply vanish. Classrooms could be designed that are all things to all children. They could be elaboratively rich for everyone; provide strategy training for everyone; support a wide range of intellectual abilities; foster respect for contributions from each individual; and teach future voting and taxpaying citizens how to cooperatively design and manage joint projects of great importance to all.[20]

NEW DIRECTIONS FOR INFORMATION PROCESSING RESEARCH

Over the past two decades, thousands of studies have been conducted using information processing paradigms. Despite a number of attempts to pull them together, the studies have not, alas, yielded a coherent picture of learning disabilities.[21] There are two main reasons for this.

First, most researchers have studied samples of children who were classified as learning-disabled by schools. As we saw in Chapter 1, classification criteria vary widely from school to school, and are often informal. The most these children have in common is low achievement in the classroom. An unlimited number of factors contribute to low achievement, and information processing research has identified some of them. But there is no way of knowing how many truly learning-disabled children, if any, were included in the research samples in the first place. To overcome this problem, researchers today are beginning to use their own criteria for defining learning-disabled children. They screen children who have been classified as learning-disabled by the school, and exclude from their experiments those who don't meet their research criteria.

The second reason why information-processing research over the past two decades has not produced a coherent picture is that researchers hold widely varying theoretical assumptions and study very different tasks. There is often no way of knowing what one set of research results has to do with another. Even when researchers use the same terms—such as perception, recognition, memory, retrieval processes, verbal abilities—they often define them quite differently. Assuming that the terms are equivalent is again an instance of the process transfer fallacy, the tacit assumption that the mental processes involved in one task will operate in the same way in other tasks. The fallacy plagues theoretical papers and research reviews as well as experimental reports.

Much information processing research is still characterized by the assumption that mental processes have a functional integrity of their own, regardless of the particular task they are "embodied" in. The assumption is less explicit than it used to be, but it remains pervasive. Today, instead of referring to these processes in terms popularized by Frostig or by Kirk, researchers refer to them in terms popularized by information processing theory—short-term memory, metacognitive abilities, elaborative processes, working memory strategies, and the like.

Psychologists and educators must continually remind themselves that these processes can be defined only in terms of particular tasks. Short-term memory cannot be defined in the abstract: there is only short-term memory *for* something, under particular conditions. A child may have a poor short-term memory for some materials, but an excellent short-term memory for others. There is not yet an overarching theory of short-term memory that would account for such phenomena, in the sense that an equation like $e=mc^2$ accounts for processes embodied in many different kinds of matter.

Contemporary information processing researchers are

therefore beginning to conduct in-depth studies of particular tasks, and to work out theoretical models of exactly how the mental processes involved in a particular task might map onto those involved in other tasks. Out of this research will grow detailed specifications of the exact conditions under which a child's mental processes may be defective, and the exact conditions under which they function well.

5/ Neuropsychological Research

Neuropsychology is the study of brain-behavior relationships.[1] It has both clinical and basic research specializations. Clinical neuropsychology arose prior to the invention of modern brain-scanning technologies. In some cases, for example, it was necessary to try to infer the location of an injury from a patient's behavior, so a neurosurgeon would know where to operate. In other cases, given a known injury, it was necessary to predict the behavioral impairments that the patient was likely to sustain. Some clinical psychologists therefore made themselves expert in neurology and specialized in brain-behavior diagnostic techniques. Today the field of clinical neuropsychology has broadened to include a pediatric specialization.[2] Brain-behavior researchers are also investigating nonclinical areas of psychology, such as perception, development, attention, and memory. These emerging fields are called developmental neuropsychology, neuropsychology of perception, cognitive neuropsychology, and so on.[3]

Neuropsychology is of special significance to learning disabilities. P.L. 94-142 defines learning disabilities as disorders which "include conditions which have been referred to as perceptual handicaps, brain injury, minimal brain dysfunction, dyslexia, developmental aphasia, etc." The National Joint Committee for Learning Disabilities defined learning disabilities as a "generic term that refers to a heterogeneous group of disorders . . . presumed to be due to central nervous system dysfunction." The Committee stated that no child should be classified as learning-disabled unless there was evidence of central nervous system involvement. What should that evidence be?

Answering that question is a central feature of neuropsychological research into learning disabilities. Except in severe cases, the evidence must be inferred from behavior. The neurological impairments that underlie learning disabilities are usually not visible on CAT scans or the results of other imaging devices. Neuropsychological researchers must therefore work out special techniques for inferring brain disorders from behavioral disorders.

The research that I will review here falls into three categories: research on neuropsychology test batteries; research on hemispheric anomalies; and research on cognitive impairments in patients with known brain injuries.

NEUROPSYCHOLOGICAL TESTS

I will trace the evolution of one particular neuropsychological test battery, as an illustration of where such tests come from and what they are expected to do.

A pioneer in the field of neuropsychological testing was Alexander Luria, late of the University of Moscow.[4] Luria had degrees in both medicine and education and contributed to numerous branches of psychology, although he is best known in the United States for his work in clinical neuropsychology. Luria developed an extensive series of informal tests for inferring the locus of brain dysfunction from a patient's behavior. In Michael Cole's description, "His neuropsychological techniques

. . . represented a highly selected set of tools fashioned from his early research on hidden psychological processes or the dynamics of cognitive development. Their validity derived in part from the intricate pattern of the whole, woven from an unprecedented span of observations, into which they fit."[5]

When Luria examined a patient, he would sometimes appear to construct tests on the spot to probe areas of dysfunction. He would follow up each test with a further test, progressively narrowing his focus. He was guided always by his knowledge of the interconnectivity of the brain, as illustrated by the diagram in Figure 12, taken from one of his books.[6]

By studying patients with known areas of impairment, Luria determined how particular "constellations" (his term) of brain cells entered into tasks like reading and drawing. The frontal lobes, for example, are involved in switching attention, and in constructing working memory programs (as we would now term them) for specific tasks. A patient with frontal lobe damage may make the kinds of errors shown in Figure 13.[7] The patient was asked to draw a circle, then a square, then a circle, and so on. Once the patient started drawing squares, he couldn't stop. (The term for this is "perseveration.")

Luria explained that the problem arose not just from damage to the frontal lobe area itself, but also from the destruction of connections to other areas. In this particular case, correct performance of the task involved connections to the auditory area. The patient had to hold a spoken word ("circle") in mind, and then compare the drawing he produced to the verbal specification. That was what this particular patient could not do. If Luria changed the task so that it activated connections to the visual area, rather than to the auditory area—by having the patient copy figures rather than draw them from dictation—the perseveration disappeared.

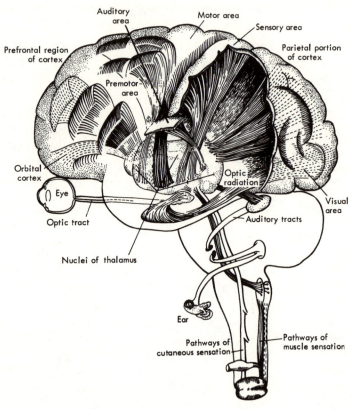

Figure 12. Luria's diagram of brain connections.

Another type of test that Luria used is shown in Figure 14. The patient was asked to reproduce the specimen pattern. The patterns labeled *a* through *e* show the errors the patient made until he finally succeeded in tracing the pattern correctly (*f*). This patient also suffered from frontal lobe damage, but in areas that were connected to his optic system rather than to his auditory system.

Over many years, Luria assembled an extensive collection of informal tests that he used to diagnose brain

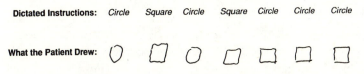

Figure 13. Drawings by patient with frontal lobe tumor.

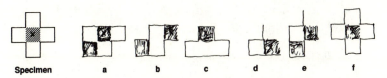

Figure 14. Successive attempts of a patient to trace a checkerboard pattern.

injury and to illustrate his theories of brain function. But these tests were not standardized. There was no way of systematically comparing a patient's test performance to the performance of normal people, or to the performance of people who had other types of brain injury. In the mid-1970s, a group of neuropsychologists at the University of Nebraska, Charles Golden, Arnold Purisch, and Thomas Hammeke, collated some of Luria's informal tests into a battery and standardized it. This is called the Luria-Nebraska Neuropsychological Battery, and it has both adult and child versions.[8]

It is very important to adjust neuropsychological tests to take account of development. For example, it would be perfectly normal for a young child to "disconnect" the motor activities of drawing from verbal instructions. We should not infer that such developmental disconnections signify brain impairment. Luria himself was very interested in development, and constructed his theory to take account of both phylogenetic and ontogenetic brain growth.[9]

The children's version of the Luria-Nebraska test is organized into eleven scales: Motor, Rhythm, Tactile, Visual, Receptive Speech, Expressive Speech, Writing, Reading, Arithmetic, Memory, and Intellectual Processes. Responses to each test item are scored 0, 1, or 2, with higher scores indicating dysfunction. These scores are summed. A child is classified as having an impairment if his scores are high (for his age) on at least two of the scales. The test administrator also interprets the child's performance qualitatively, the way Luria did.

APPLICATIONS TO LEARNING DISABILITIES

One might expect a test like the Luria-Nebraska to constitute the ideal way of detecting and diagnosing learning-disabled children. It should discriminate learning-disabled children from nondisabled children, as well as pinpoint the location of the brain dysfunction. As it has turned out, however, the Luria-Nebraska doesn't discriminate learning-disabled children any better than other tests do—particularly the combination of IQ and achievement tests that most schools use. The scales in the Luria-Nebraska cluster into three types: tests of sensorimotor abilities, tests of thinking, and tests of academic achievement. The tests of thinking amount to an IQ test, but it turns out not to be as good as the IQ test that most schools use (the WISC-R), nor are the Luria-Nebraska tests of academic achievement as good as others that are available (the Woodcock-Johnson tests, for example). The sensorimotor tests in the Luria-Nebraska are not useful in discriminating learning-disabled children; a child's ability to manipulate pegs, or to copy a geometric form, simply has nothing to do with his ability to read or spell.[10]

A further disappointment of the Luria-Nebraska is that it has not proved successful in pinpointing special characteristics of a child's brain dysfunction. It is not possible to say, on the basis of a child's test protocol, that she has "frontal lobe disconnections to the auditory system" (like the patient of Figure 13) or "frontal lobe disconnections to the visual system" (Figure 14). People who administer the test may make such interpretations, but it is not possible to know, for sure, if they are correct.

Finally, the Luria-Nebraska is not based on current theories of brain development. For example, the test assumes that the frontal lobes do not mature until adolescence.[11] This is contrary to contemporary research. Frontal lobes are active at a very early age, probably from birth.[12]

Overall, this apparently promising approach to the diagnosis of learning disabilities has not turned out to be very useful. In my judgment, the same story can be told about all neuropsychological tests. There are many of them, and many additional clinical methods (informal interpretative methods) of trying to pinpoint what may be going wrong in a child's brain. But in fact it may be impossible ever to know, from a child's response to a test question, how the brain contrived to produce that response. The most a behavioral test may ever be able to do is show us that something is wrong, relative to the performance of a sample of children the same age, and to tell us whether or not similar difficulties are likely to appear on other tests—school tests, for example.

However, research into neuropsychological test construction is proceeding apace, and accurate methods of inferring brain dysfunction from test behaviors may someday emerge. If they do, they will probably be derived from experimental and clinical studies of the sort to be described next.

HEMISPHERIC VARIATIONS

Ever since Orton, researchers have been investigating the possibility that learning disabilities could arise from hemispheric "imbalances," specifically (according to

Orton) from the failure of the left hemisphere to become dominant for reading and writing.

Methods of assessing the relative contributions of the two hemispheres to tasks such as reading and writing are based on how the brain is "wired" to hands and eyes, as sketched in Figure 15.[13]

Areas of each hemisphere are specialized for receiving sensory information and for sending motor commands. But, for complicated evolutionary reasons that we won't go into here, each hemisphere is in part wired to the opposite half of the body. The left hemisphere controls the right half of the body; the right hemisphere controls the left half. This is true for limbs and for eyes, as shown in Figure 15. (The hemispheres also exert some control over same-side functions, but we need not go into that.)

The right hemisphere is connected to the left visual field, not simply to the left eye. Similarly, the left hemisphere is connected to the right visual field. To understand what a visual field is, hold a pencil in front of you at arm's length and focus on its point. Your left and right eyes are both picking up information to the right of the point. That is your right visual field. Your left and right eyes are also both picking up information to the left of the point. That is your left visual field.

Brain-body wiring suggests that if a particular side of the body is dominant for some activity, like handwriting, then the opposite hemisphere may be controlling it. Therefore, if a right-handed person has poor handwriting, the left hemisphere may be weak or somehow impaired. The problem with this hypothesis is that the two hemispheres are normally connected by a bridge of fibers called the corpus callosum. Neural activity in one hemisphere is swiftly transmitted to the other hemisphere over this bridge. In a complex task such as writing, uncountable numbers of such exchanges occur. The rel-

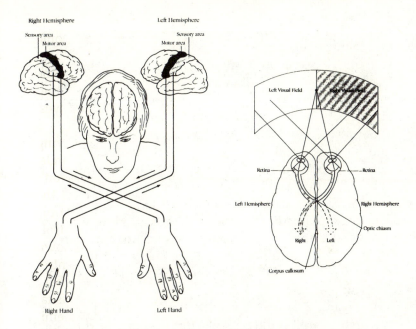

Figure 15. How the brain is wired to the hands and eyes.

ative contribution of each hemisphere can therefore only be studied by special techniques.

SPLIT-BRAIN STUDIES

In cases of extremely severe epilepsy, where patients are in a chronic seizure state and all attempts at medication have failed, a brain operation called a commissurotomy is occasionally performed. Portions of the corpus callosum and certain other connecting fibers are severed. This helps prevent the epileptic discharge or "storm" from spreading across the brain. Patients who have received this operation are known as split-brain patients.[14]

In split-brain patients, information cannot be directly transmitted from one hemisphere to the other in the normal, swift fashion. Thus it is possible to study how each hemisphere performs various tasks such as reading, drawing, labeling, and categorizing. A study conducted by Jerre Levy and Colwyn Trevarthen was of special interest to me, because I had conducted a developmental study in 1975 that explored similar questions.[15]

Suppose a child is shown three pictures—a cat, a dog, and a book—and is asked: "Which two belong together?" The dog and the cat are both brown; the book is red. The dog and the cat are about the same size, and are standing in profile. The book is rectangular, lying flat. The child points to the dog and the cat. How was the judgment made? On the basis of color, form, function, or all three? The results of my study suggested that five-year-olds, like adults, base their judgment largely on form similarities.

Levy and Trevarthen used a similar method in their research on split-brain patients. But they put the question to each hemisphere separately. The answer from the right hemisphere: form. The answer from the left hemisphere: function. The study confirms what has been concluded from a large number of other studies, that the right hemisphere is specialized for dealing with patterns as wholes. The left hemisphere is specialized for language and for other functions that language involves, such as analysis and classification.

Such findings have been widely popularized and often misrepresented. We hear now that some people are "left-brained" while others are "right-brained." The implication is that everything a "left-brained" person does will be characterized by language-based, analytic, categorical thought processes, while everything a "right-brained" person does will be characterized by pattern recognition and dealing with experiences as wholes. It is also said the "left brain" is logical, while the "right brain" is creative, and, most pertinently, that learning-disabled children are "right-brained" learners in "left-brained" school settings. This is all nonsense. Even in split-brain patients, the brain works as a whole on any task it is engaged in.

The only credible question regarding learning-disabled children is whether they differ from nondisabled children in the degree to which the left or right hemisphere is activated during the performance of particular tasks. There are several methods that are used to address that question.

METHODS OF STUDYING HEMISPHERIC DIFFERENCES

Three methods are most frequently used in studying relative activation of the hemispheres: visual field tasks, dichotic listening tasks, and cerebral space-sharing tasks.

Visual field tasks. Remember the pencil you were holding at arm's length, while focusing on its point? Now imagine that the room goes dark, and is then illuminated by a flash of light. Assume you are still staring at the pencil point. During the instant of the light flash, there isn't time for information to pass between the hemispheres. Only your left hemisphere registers what's in your right visual field, and only your right hemisphere registers what's in your left visual field. By varying materials flashed to each visual field, researchers can tell what the hemispheres are specialized for. It turns out that the right hemisphere is better (quicker and more accurate) at recognizing faces and at remembering dot patterns. The left hemisphere is better at recognizing letters and words.[16]

Dichotic listening studies. Individuals may display right or left ear specializations for certain types of stimuli. In the dichotic listening method, stimuli are presented through earphones to both ears simultaneously. Which ear best hears certain types of sounds? If listeners are told to attend to one ear, can they do it? Can they switch to the other ear efficiently? The results of such studies suggest that the right ear (left hemisphere) is specialized for verbal stimuli like words and numbers, while the left ear (right hemisphere) is specialized for nonverbal stimuli like music.[17] However, a number of factors can influence these effects. For example, only untrained musicians show the left ear (right hemisphere) superiority for music; trained musicians show a left-hemispheric superiority.[18] Since trained musicians are likely to be more analytic, this finding supports the analytic-holistic distinction. It also shows that hemispheric involvement in a task can be altered by learning. Another series of studies showed that even short-term learning can alter the superiority of the right ear (left hemisphere) for processing verbal stimuli. Children were asked to attend to one ear, and report the spoken numbers that were heard by that ear. Then they were asked to attend to the other ear. The right-ear superiority for numbers was sharply reduced if the children had practiced attending to the left ear first. This "priming" effect persisted for days.[19]

Cerebral space-sharing studies. This technique was developed by Marcel Kinsbourne, of Brandeis University and Harvard Medical School. It uses the dual-task paradigm explained in Chapter 4. Kinsbourne theorized that if two tasks are handled primarily by the same hemisphere, they would interfere with each other. If each task is performed by a different hemisphere, interference should be less.[20] His hypothesis was supported. In one study, children tapped a table while reciting a nursery rhyme. Disruption of the tasks was greater when the children tapped with their right hands; the right hand is connected more strongly to the left hemisphere, which is specialized for language.[21]

APPLICATIONS TO THE STUDY OF LEARNING DISABILITIES

If differences in hemispheric specialization and task involvement are at the root of learning disabilities, then learning-disabled children should be different from non-disabled children on tasks like the ones just described. Yet very often they are not, and when they are, the difference is difficult to interpret.[22]

John Obrzut, of the University of Arizona, studied learning-disabled and nondisabled ten-year-olds.[23] He administered a battery of tests, looking for those that would discriminate most sharply between the two groups. He found that a test of dichotic listening was the best discriminator.

The children listened to syllables ("ba," "da," etc.) through earphones. On some of the trials, they were directed to report what they heard in the left ear; on other trials, in the right. (The ear was touched repeatedly, so the children understood which ear was meant.) The results of such studies are reported in terms of what is called the Right Ear Advantage (REA). The scores of the left ear (right hemisphere) are subtracted from the scores of the right ear (left hemisphere). As noted above, the right ear (left hemisphere) is usually better on verbal materials, even when you are trying to attend to the left ear. Therefore, the REA is usually positive. The results of Obrzut's study are shown in Table 4.

The nondisabled children displayed the typical positive REA, no matter which ear they were supposed to be reporting. The learning-disabled children, on the other hand, were much better at switching their attention. When attending to the right ear, their REA score was +12. When attending to the left, it was −3. That is, they were better at following the instructions than the nondisabled children were.

What are we to make of these findings? They certainly

Table 4. Right Ear Advantage (REA) Scores for Learning-Disabled and Nondisabled Children

	Average REAs	
Directions	Nondisabled	Learning-Disabled
"Report whatever you heard . . ." (30 trials)	+3	+5
"Report right ear . . ." (30 trials)	+3	+12
"Report left ear . . ." (30 trials)	+3	−3

don't show that learning-disabled children have weak left-hemispheric dominance, nor that they favor their right hemispheres. If that were the case, the learning-disabled children would have had lower REA scores than the nondisabled children did. That is, their right ear (left hemisphere) scores would have been relatively poor. This pattern did not appear. On the contrary, the REA scores of the learning-disabled children were higher than those of the nondisabled children, except when the children were specifically instructed to favor the other ear.

Hence, although the learning-disabled children were different from the nondisabled children, the difference favored the learning-disabled group. They were more efficient, mentally, than the nondisabled children. Does it make sense to theorize that such a difference underlies poor reading, writing, and arithmetic performance in school?

It has been speculated that the greater ear-switching efficiencies of learning-disabled children could signify weaker connections between the hemispheres, perhaps some missing or impaired fibers in the corpus callosum.[24] But research that more directly explores this possibility has not been conclusive.[25]

What it all seems to come down to is that hemispheric differences in themselves cannot account for learning disabilities. To account for the disabilities, some underlying neurological dysfunction (like a damaged corpus callosum) must be postulated. It is this underlying dysfunction which may cause both the hemispheric differences and the disabled behaviors. In the words of Merrill Hicks and Marcel Kinsbourne:

> Deviant patterns of functional organization within a healthy, intact brain are not maladaptive. When cognitive deficit is associated with deviant cerebral organization, both anomalies probably stem from injury to the brain which may be attributed, in turn, to either exogenous or endogenous factors. . . . In general, the neural basis of learning disorders appears to be brain pathology rather than anomalous brain organization per se, but the nature of the pathology remains a matter of speculation.[26]

COGNITIVE NEUROPSYCHOLOGY

During the 1960s and early 1970s, as information processing theories were being developed, a group of British psychologists began to use these theories to interpret the cognitive losses of brain-damaged patients. It soon became clear that the behavior of these patients had important implications for the theories themselves, and a new field called cognitive neuropsychology was launched.

Its guiding assumptions are the following: Suppose a cognitive theory specifies distinctions between certain mental functions. If a case can be located where one of these functions has been impaired while the others remain intact, then support for the distinctions has been obtained. For example, if cognitive theory specifies that working memory and long-term memory are separate components of the mind, and an injury selectively impairs working memory, leaving long-term memory intact, then this supports the theory that the two memories are structurally and functionally distinct. It also has important rehabilitation implications for the patient. Such hypotheses are tested by means of intensive studies of single cases.

THE CASE OF K.F.

A famous case in the field of cognitive neuropsychology is that of a patient known as K.F. He was studied by Elizabeth Warrington and Tim Shallice at the Institute of Neurology at the National Hospital in London.[27]

K.F. suffered a severe head injury from a motorcycle accident when he was seventeen years old. He remained unconscious for ten weeks. After five months, he could walk unaided, but could say only a few words. After fifteen months he could carry on a conversation, but was still unable to read or write. He began to have seizures a few months later, and an operation was performed to excise scar tissue that was causing the seizures. The location of the damage is shown in Figure 16. The angular gyrus (the part of the brain thought to be impaired in dyslexia) is just above and behind the coiled artery.[28]

Warrington and Shallice administered a series of tests to K.F., including an IQ test. He had a verbal IQ of 79 and a performance IQ of 113, indicating that his verbal abilities were selectively impaired. His digit span score (the number of spoken numerals he could recall) was 2 at best; on some trials he could not repeat more than 1 digit, and on other trials, none. Warrington and Shallice systematically narrowed down the exact nature of this working memory problem by administering tests which answered a series of questions.

Did the problem result from faulty auditory perception? The answer was no, on the basis of the following tests: (a) Repeating the last digit in series of various

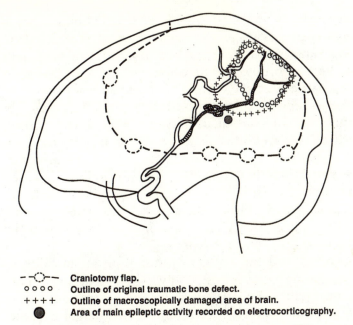

- ‑‑◯‑‑ **Craniotomy flap.**
- ◦◦◦◦ **Outline of original traumatic bone defect.**
- ++++ **Outline of macroscopically damaged area of brain.**
- ● **Area of main epileptic activity recorded on electrocorticography.**

Figure 16. Areas of brain dysfunction in patient K.F.

lengths there was no evidence of increased confusion from longer strings. (b) Matching: "Are these the same? Four thirty-eight, four fifty-eight." K.F. made very few errors. (c) Recognizing a particular number or letter that was repeated in a 20-item list; K.F. tapped the table each time he heard the target item. He made only 2 errors in 160 trials. (d) Category recognition: K.F. tapped when he heard an item that belonged to a particular category (animal, color, country, and so on). Again, K.F. made only 2 errors. On these particular measures, then, his auditory perception appeared to be unimpaired.

Next, did the problem result from articulation damage? K.F. did have some difficulty speaking. Was this why his digit span was subnormal? The answer was no, on the basis of the following tests: (a) Pointing: K.F.'s digit span was just as short when he pointed to numbers on an answer card as when he spoke the numbers aloud. (b) Part-reporting: K.F. repeated the first or second item of a pair of items. He was not told in advance which he was to repeat. Although he had to hold both items in mind, he had to articulate only one of them. The reduced articulation requirements did not help; he still could not hold both items in mind reliably. (c) Vocalization: K.F. repeated each digit as it was presented to him, and then attempted to recall the set. This procedure actually helped. On three-digit strings, he was able to repeat seven out of twenty correctly; on four-digit strings, he repeated three out of twenty correctly.

Finally, did the problem result from an inability to learn (as opposed to an inability to hold items in working memory for brief periods)? The answer was no, on the basis of the following tests: (a) K.F. was taught ten pairs of words, practicing each three times. The average score of fifty normal subjects in K.F.'s age range was 15.7 (out of 30); K.F.'s score was 14.5. (b) K.F. was taught a list of ten words. He repeated them as best he could, until he was able to recite all ten correctly. He needed seven trials. Twenty normal controls took an average of nine trials, and four of them were unable to learn the list, even after twenty trials. Two months later, K.F. could recall seven of the ten words without relearning.

IMPLICATIONS FOR LEARNING DISABILITIES

Studies of patients like K.F. have important implications for the field of learning disabilities. To begin with, they chart ways in which neurological damage can selectively impair mental processes. The degree of specificity is often astonishing, given the extent of the damage in some patients. K.F.'s memory impairment, for example, was limited to auditory-verbal materials. (Another experiment showed that K.F.'s memory span for environmental sounds, like the barking of dogs, was not impaired.)[29] K.F.'s problem was further narrowed to the buffer level in our schema of information processing. He could take in the information (feature detection) and once it was transferred from buffer to working memory he could speak it (behavior output), and he could transfer it to long-term memory (learn). What he could not do was hold it in short-term memory (buffer it). That suggests that there may be a buffer that is exclusively specialized for speech sounds.

In that case, might the selective impairment of a speech sound buffer also be characteristic of some learning-disabled children? Do these children have particular difficulty learning to read, write, and spell? Such hypotheses have turned out to be fruitful.

6/ A Dyslexic Boy Grows Up

When we turn from the search for generalized dysfunctions to the search for dysfunctions on specific school tasks, the research picture becomes clearer. The main defining feature of a learning disability is specificity. A child with a learning disability is a child who has unusual difficulties on some school tasks, but not on others. This specificity is what distinguishes a learning disability from general retardation.

In the majority of cases, learning disabilities are specific to reading and writing. Sometimes, but not always, the child will display similar difficulties with speech. He may get tangled up in syntax when he talks as well as when he writes. Such disorders have been recognized medically for a long time, and are termed *dyslexia* (referring to reading), *dysgraphia* (writing and spelling), and *aphasia* (understanding and producing speech). This chapter presents the case of a young man for whom we have a detailed educational history.

Dave is now twenty-two years old. He is completing a college degree in a highly competitive area—business administration with a specialization in finance—with a B+ average. As part of his training, Dave interned in a financial office, where he wrote a documentation manual for a computer program in financial analysis, work that was pronounced excellent by his supervisors.

We have a succession of test records on Dave. He was tested in second grade, eighth grade, high school, and at the beginning and end of college. The records reveal the specificity of Dave's disorder, and also provide glimpses of his developing character, especially his growing determination to succeed.

TEST RECORDS

SECOND GRADE

By 1976, when Dave was almost eight years old, it had become clear that he had a reading problem. He was referred for testing because, according to the referral notes, there seemed to be "a serious gap between his reading level and his academic ability" in other areas. Dave was reading at the primer level, and "he cannot seem to remember words. However, he understands and speaks at a higher level. Eye-hand coordination is good, and number level is 2nd grade."[1]

At that time, P.L. 94-142 was just beginning to be implemented. The new term "learning disability" was used with reference to Dave (although he was never formally classified as learning-disabled by the public school system) and the discrepancies between his intelligence and his reading ability were noted. On a picture vocabulary test that measured verbal intelligence, Dave displayed a mental age that was three years ahead of his chronological age. However, this clearly bright child was not learning to read.

In an attempt to diagnose his problem, Dave was given tests derived from the processing theories described in

Chapter 3. The tests included one for hemispheric dominance (Dave was perfectly normal); two tests of the "visual channel," including the Frostig test of visual forms and a test of memory for designs (Dave excelled on these); two tests of the "auditory channel"—recognition of similar-sounding word pairs, and repeating back random numbers (Dave performed the first with ease, but had difficulties with the second, an important clue); two arithmetic tests (Dave performed overall at the appropriate grade level); and seven reading tests. In Table 5, I have collated the reading tests that were administered again as Dave grew up.

In second grade, Dave was quite able to recognize letter patterns in isolation. But when the letters were put together in words, he could not recognize the words. He had not learned letter-sound correspondences (as revealed by his inability to sound out nonsense words) and his understanding of word and paragraph meanings was commensurately poor. The examiner found these reading deficiencies puzzling: "Dave would seem to have all the necessary skills to read: auditory discrimination, left-right discrimination, ability to recognize and print letters, visual perception, verbal intelligence, and visual memory."

Table 5. Dave's Grade Levels (Woodcock Reading Mastery Test)

Subtest	Age 7 (grade 2)	Age 13 (grade 8)	Age 17 (grade 12)
Letter Identification (letters in isolation)	2.4	12.9	—
Word Identification	1.6	3.4	3.7
Word Attack (sounding out nonsense words)	1.6	2.0	2.5
Word Comprehension	1.4	5.5	—
Passage Comprehension	1.8	6.4	6.7

A conclusion very often drawn from such findings is that other factors—typically, the child's lack of motivation, or family problems—are causing the child's reading failure. Fortunately, Dave's wise examiner, who tested him from second grade through high school, did not burden Dave and his family with these implications. As Dave reflects upon it today: "They knew something was wrong, they knew I couldn't help it, but they didn't know what to do about it."

Dave was not formally classified as learning-disabled, and did not receive special services from his school, since the only available services were for slow-learning children. (This is often the case.) However, the school did provide Dave's parents with some supplemental homework materials, and suggested private tutoring. The possibility of retaining Dave in second grade was discussed but rejected, and Dave moved ahead with his class.

EIGHTH GRADE

The eighth-grade evaluation was initiated by Dave's language arts teacher, who according to the examiner

> feels a possible perceptual problem exists, as Dave at times reverses his letters and leaves off word endings [in both reading and writing]. However, he is able to perform well orally . . . [and] his academics are described as above level. Dave is described as a very conscientious young man who completes all his classwork with acceptable peer relationships and above average maturity. He is a very quiet shy boy who works in a slouching manner, and who the teacher feels does not want to seem to draw attention to himself.

The examiner observed Dave in a science class and reported:

> He entered the classroom and went directly to his seat and spoke quietly to the two boys seated at the table with

him. When the class started he opened his book to the appropriate page and seemed interested in the lesson. The students read questions completed previously and their answers. Dave did not raise his hand to participate in this activity. On one occasion later, he did volunteer but that was when he could provide a one-word response and not be required to read aloud. The students then participated in an experiment and Dave seemed highly interested in what was going on.

The reason for Dave's reticence is clear from Table 5. Although he could now perfectly recognize letters in isolation (12.9 is the highest grade level), he could recognize words only at a third-grade level, and his Word Attack skills were even lower. Remarkably, however, Dave was somehow getting the meaning of words and passages. This was shown not only by his comprehension test scores, but also by his grades, which were consistently good. Dave spent hours completing his reading and writing homework, and had worked out strategies for dealing with it. For example, he would memorize the exact spelling of technical terms in science.

It was again decided not to classify Dave as learning-disabled, but arrangements were made for him to have resource room assistance with reading and writing. Like the second-grade report, which ended with expressing concern that Dave would have difficulty with later grades in elementary school, the eighth-grade report expressed concern that Dave would have difficulty in high school. Nevertheless, there seemed nothing to do but pass him along.

HIGH SCHOOL

As it turned out, Dave graduated second in his high school class, having been enrolled in honors physics, pre-calculus, and college-bound English. Yet, as Table 5 shows, his twelfth-grade reading test scores were still extremely low. At the age of seventeen, he could recognize words only at the third-grade level, his Word Attack skills remained at the second-grade level, and his Passage Comprehension skills—on this particular test—had not progressed beyond the sixth-grade level. However, Dave was clearly able to acquire information at a much higher level.

Dave's special skills and determination were strikingly illustrated by the fact that he was made a field coach, then a field conductor, and finally drum major of his high school marching band. This position is notable for the number of patterns that must be kept track of simultaneously—movement patterns, musical patterns, and rhythmic patterns. Additionally, extraordinary precision and self-discipline are required. (As it happens, I am a drum corps fanatic, even to the point of traveling to the national competitions, and have thought a lot about the skills involved.) Dave led his band to regional championships and won a number of personal awards. Most important, as Dave reflects upon it today, his marching band experiences forced him to overcome his feelings of shyness and his fear of making mistakes in public. "I think," he says of his relationship with the band director, "that I was the most yelled-at conductor ever." What helped him through it was the support of the band members, who found him to be an excellent coach and liked him personally. By his senior year, Dave was a widely popular high school star.

Throughout high school, Dave received special help from his English teachers, but he was never classified as learning-disabled. He took the Scholastic Aptitude Test under regular (timed) conditions, and achieved respectable scores: 470 on the verbal section, and 560 on the mathematics section. He was accepted into several colleges, and chose the University of Delaware. By this time, his teachers were no longer predicting academic doom for Dave. He had proved them wrong too many times. The twelfth-grade report ended with the prediction that Dave would succeed in college, as indeed he has.

COLLEGE

When Dave arrived at the University of Delaware, he brought a letter from his high school examiner explaining that Dave was dyslexic. We then gave him a comprehensive battery of tests. The scores in Table 6 are reported in terms of percentiles, for easy comparison. The pattern is quite clear: Dave's IQ is in the High Average range (75th percentile). His scores on tests of mathematics and general knowledge (science, social studies, and humanities) are in the 80th percentiles. His scores on tests of reading, writing, and spelling, however, range from the 2nd to the 22nd percentiles. This pattern is typical of dyslexic/dysgraphic students of all ages. It

Table 6. Dave's Test Profile

Test	Percentile
Wechsler Adult Intelligence Scale	
Verbal IQ (score: 107)	68
Performance IQ (112)	79
Full Scale IQ (110)	75
Woodcock-Johnson Psychoeducational Battery	
Reading	12
Written Language	22
Mathematics	85
Knowledge	80
Wide Range Achievement Test	
Word Recognition	2
Spelling	2

sharply reveals the specificity characteristic of these disorders.

Errors are of special importance in understanding dyslexia, because they provide clues to some of the contributing factors. There are many methods of analyzing reading and writing errors.[2] Most of the methods focus on letter-by-letter characteristics—which letter has been substituted for which, and so on. These methods have limited practical value. We have found it more useful to classify errors into three broad categories: (a) representational; (b) rule-based; and (c) word-substitution.

Representational errors reveal a failure to maintain a stable visual or aural representation of a word, for example, reading "munipal" for *municipal,* or spelling "rercin" when *reverence* was dictated. Maintaining a stable representation is the first step in reading or spelling correctly. The second step is retrieving, from memory, the letters or sounds that correspond to those patterns.

Rule-based errors show that although a stable representation was maintained, the wrong letters or sounds were retrieved, for example, pronouncing *municipal* as "munnicipal," with the accent on the first syllable, or spelling it "municiple."

Finally, there are word-substitution errors, such as reading or writing "munition" for *municipal.*

The type of errors that students make depends to some degree on their instructional program. Students have been in programs that teach letter-sound correspondences (phonics) are likely to make rule-based errors. Those in programs which have taught them to guess words from the first two or three letters are likely to make word-substitution errors. Students who have had some exposure to spelling rules usually try to spell phonetically, thus making rule-based errors. Students who were taught to rely on visual memory (by memorizing lists of words) sometimes put down whatever word or letters they can remember, producing either word-substitution or representation errors.

When Dave was in second grade, he made mostly word-substitution errors. His examiner noted that David said "have" for *here*, "come" for *can*, "came" for *come*, "bell" for *ball*, "happy" for *help*, "white" for *with*, "ran" for *ride*, "party" for *puppy*, "was" for *wish*, and "round" for *road*. The examiner also recorded some of Dave's misreadings of nonsense words. He read "men" for *mam*, "pone" for *poe*, and "nen" for *en*.

While it was recommended that Dave be given further training in word attack skills, the record doesn't show that this occurred. On the eighth-grade tests, the examiner wrote:

> Errors noted were: "unit" for *until*, "whill" for *while*, and "forked" for *front*. These errors he was able to correct when they were pointed out to him. Additional errors he was unable to correct included "quiet" for *quick*, "price" for *piece*, "brush" for *busy*, and "sloppy" for *soapy*, among others . . . The word *piece* was brought to Dave's attention and he was asked what sound the *ie* normally produces. However, he was unable to respond and appeared to be confused in relation to this request.

On the nonsense word test, Dave read "blem" for *bim*, "tat" for *kak*, and "zad" for *ziz*, among others.

The examiner concluded that while Dave apparently had some perceptual problems (reading *t* instead of *k*, for example), the major difficulty seemed to be that he had never learned basic phonics: "He seems unaware of rules relating to a single vowel in a word, two vowels together, a vowel-consonant-vowel combination, etc.

When asked simply to provide the short vowel sound, he substituted the short *a* sound for the *e*, and the short *u* sound for the *o*." The examiner recommended that Dave be taught basic phonics, beginning with primary books. However, Dave does not remember that this recommendation was implemented. The help he received in the remainder of eighth grade, and throughout the four subsequent years of high school, was directed mostly toward his school assignments.

Despite this help, Dave entered college with serious problems. Table 7 lists Dave's errors on the word recognition and spelling tests that were administered in college. They are primarily representational errors. Dave was not maintaining stable visual or aural patterns. His difficulties with school assignments are illustrated in Figure 18, a page from his first freshman history essay.

Table 7. Dave's Reading and Spelling Errors

Reading	
Printed word	*What Dave said*
deny	"dean, devee"
bibliography	"bigblaography"
unanimous	"anominous"
mosaic	"moisid"
municipal	"munipal"
deteriorate	"deforick"
Spelling	
Dictated word	*What Dave wrote*
suggestion	subjustion
equipment	equicment
majority	majuration
institute	injustion
reverence	rercin
museum	meudian

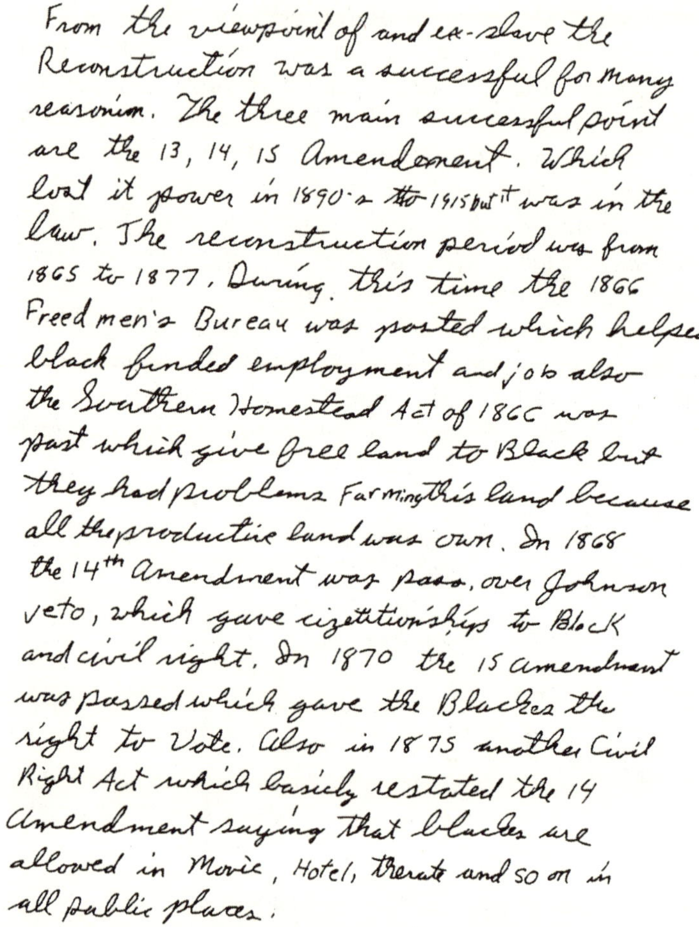

From the viewpoint of and ex-slave the Reconstruction was a successful for many reasonism. The three main successful point are the 13, 14, 15 Amendement. Which lost it power in 1890's tho 1915 but it was in the law. The reconstruction period was from 1865 to 1877. During this time the 1866 Freedmen's Bureau was posted which helped black funded employment and job also the Southern Homestead Act of 1866 was past which give free land to Black but they had problems Farming this land because all the productive land was own. In 1868 the 14th Amendment was pass. over Johnson veto, which gave cizettionships to Block and civil right. In 1870 the 15 amendment was passed which gave the Blackes the right to vote. Also in 1875 another Civil Right Act which basicly restated the 14 Amendment saying that blackes are allowed in Movie, Hotel, therate and so on in all public places.

Figure 17. Sample of writing by a dyslexic college student.

Note the anomalies that appear in the essay. In the first line, Dave wrote "and" when he meant "an"; he inserted an ungrammatical "a" before the word "successful"; he spelled "Reconstruction" correctly (he had memorized it); but then he perseverated the "ion" and appended it to "reason," producing "reasonion." In the third and fourth lines, he forgot to add *s* to pluralize "point" and "Amendement" (spelled almost correctly). The fifth line is not a sentence (it is barely understandable), and leaves the *s* off "it." In the fifth sentence, Dave wrote "pasted" when he meant "passed," and perseverated the *ed* to "finded" when he should have written "found." And so on. The ideas that Dave was trying to express were in fact quite good (he got a B+ on the essay). It seems unbelievable that someone who can acquire such complex historical information cannot remember the difference between *an* and *and,* nor a highly frequent (if irregular) past tense like *found.* This again indicates the specificity of the handicap that is dyslexia.

REMEDIATION AND ASSISTANCE

Although P.L. 94-142 does not extend to universities, another federal law does: the Rehabilitation Act of 1973. Section 504 of this act specifies that universities (and employers) are required to make "reasonable accommodations" for "otherwise qualified" students who are "handicapped." Handicapping conditions include eating disorders, psychosis, and learning disabilities, among many others.[3] Within limits, universities are permitted to work out their own definitions of "otherwise qualified" (at the University of Delaware qualification is established when a student is admitted through regular admissions procedures, as Dave was), "learning-disabled" (Dave was finally classified as learning-disabled on the basis of the tests administered at the University of Delaware), and "reasonable accommodations."

Dave has received handicapped-student services throughout his college career. They have included free tutoring, extensive personal counseling and advising, and special arrangements for course examinations. Dave may, if he chooses (he doesn't always), take his course examinations in a private room with a proctor who verifies he has read the test questions correctly, helps him spell the words he wants to use, and makes sure his sentences are legible. Dave, incidentally, does not like to take examinations orally. He prefers to write them, for the same reason that many people do—it helps him organize and clarify his ideas. All of Dave's professors have been unfailingly cooperative.

Dave's major field of study does not require a foreign language. If it had, Dave (knowing Dave) would probably have given it a try, and he might well have been successful. It is by no means the case that all dyslexics are unable to learn a foreign language. To some extent, English is a foreign language for dyslexics, and often the strategies they invent for dealing with English serve them well in learning a new language—especially if the script is different, as in Russian or Chinese. However, if dyslexics turn out to have difficulty learning a foreign language, the university permits them to take alternative courses in the culture and history of a foreign nation.

In addition to these general services, we placed Dave in a remedial reading and writing course designed especially for dyslexic college students.

INTENSIVE LITERACY

The program is based on principles developed originally by Samuel Orton. Working with Orton in the 1930s were three brilliant teachers, Anna Gillingham, Beth Slingerland, and Romalda Spalding. Gillingham, with Bessie Stillman, developed what came to be known as the Orton-Gillingham tutoring method.[4] Slingerland, recognizing the labor-intensive limitations of tutoring, developed a whole-class instructional method for learning-disabled children based on Orton's principles.[5] Spalding had in the meantime discovered that her dyslexic students, who were taught by Orton's methods, learned to read better than her normal students did. She devised a whole-class Orton-based method for normal children. Her objective was to prevent reading problems from developing in the first place.[6]

The program we call Intensive Literacy incorporates components of all three methods and adds some contemporary scientific principles. It is designed for all age levels. The program begins by teaching letter-sound units, called phonograms, in isolation. The student learns, for example, that the letters *th* have two sounds, unvoiced (as in *thin*) and voiced (as in *this*). The sounds are learned together, in order of frequency (the unvoiced sound is more frequent). The students write phonograms from dictation and read them aloud from cards. Four or five phonograms are learned at a time, and cumulatively reviewed at each lesson. They are extensively practiced. This overlearning (as it is technically termed) automates recognition and retrieval of letter-sound units.

After about fifty phonograms have been learned, students begin spelling. They are taught a strict procedure. The word (for example, *mother*) is dictated, and the student is asked: "How many syllables? . . . First syllable: What's the first sound you say?" (Not "What letter does it begin with?") The student says the sound, and the instructor then says: "Now, write it." Thus the student learns a procedure for breaking a word into syllables, breaking the syllables into phonemes, and sequentially retrieving from memory the letters associated with those phonemes. Students then read, again and again, the lists of words they have spelled. Each class begins with cumulative review.

During spelling lessons, students are gradually introduced to rules (about twenty of them), such as the rule that a silent *e* at the end of a word causes the vowel to take its long (open) sound. Additionally, students learn a simple marking system for showing what rules a word is following. For example, the word *mother* would be marked by dividing it into two syllables; underlining *th* and *er* to show that they are phonograms, not blends; and putting a 2 over *th* to show that it takes its second most frequent sound. The marked word would appear like this:

2
moth er

Students mark hundreds of words, gradually compiling a glossary of marked words in a notebook. Needless to say, college students quickly begin bringing technical terms from other courses to their Intensive Literacy classes, and after verifying their markings, add the words to their personal glossaries.

Nothing so far has been said about reading.[7] In fact students have been reading and rereading lists of spelled words, and building a coded sight vocabulary through marking practice. Their analytical so-called phonics lessons ("phonics" is a hopelessly muddled term that I try to avoid using) are conducted entirely during spelling lessons, not during reading. It interrupts the flow of reading to stop and analyze words. In Intensive Literacy classes, students read for meaning and for pleasure. During reading practice, class discussion is about the author's intention, the connection between ideas, the main point of a paragraph, and so on. If a student stumbles over a word, the instructor quickly writes the marked word on the blackboard. At a glance, the student sees how it should be pronounced, and can continue, with minimal interruption, his train of thought.

Overall, then, the Intensive Literacy program has automatic components, analytical components, and strategy components. On the automatic level, the program drills alphabetic units (phonograms), handwriting (word processing is taught elsewhere in the university), and word recognition. On the analytical level, the program teaches close attention to graphic and sound details, and techniques for decomposing and recomposing alphabetic units. On the strategy level, the program teaches techniques for summarizing, remembering, and integrating ideas.

DAVE'S PROGRESS IN READING

Dave has attended Intensive Literacy classes (which meet three hours a week) throughout his college career. Additionally, he has had many private tutoring sessions with Intensive Literacy instructors.

The first sign of reading improvement is often that a student begins to read for pleasure. This happened with Dave. During the summer following his freshman year, after two semesters of Intensive Literacy, Dave began reading straight through the novels of Stephen King. (He's still at it!)

College reading material has become progressively easier for Dave, especially in areas of his specialization, where he has become familiar with subject matter and technical jargon. He reports that reading feels easier and less stressful for him. As his grade point average (approaching 3.5) signifies, Dave is clearly learning from text material.

What about Dave's performance on standardized tests? In Table 8, we reprint some of Dave's earlier reading test scores, along with his final scores from tests administered recently. Dave is still not very good at reading words by themselves, or at spelling, but he has become spectacularly good at comprehending words in context. How does he do it?

Table 8. Dave's Standardized Reading Test Scores

Test	Age 7	Age 13	Age 17	Age 22
Woodcock Reading Mastery Test				
Word Identification	1.6	3.4	3.7	4.7
Word Attack	1.6	2.0	2.5	3.6
Passage Comprehension	1.8	6.4	6.7	12.9[a]
Wide Range Achievement Test				
Word Recognition	—	—	5B	7E
Spelling	—	—	4B	5B

B=beginning level of grade; E=end.
a. Highest score possible.

Table 9 provides some clues. It shows errors that Dave made on the word reading test administered when he entered college, and four years later. While some misperceptions are still occurring, Dave has learned to pick up more of a word, more of its letter-sound units. These apparently small improvements in Dave's decoding skills have made a tremendous difference in his comprehension skills: they give him a much better chance of activating the correct meaning of a word. Additionally, Dave has worked hard to improve his comprehension strategies—for example, to ask himself continuously if a text is making sense, if it is consistent. All this takes time, and Dave reads slowly and laboriously. But he can now read anything he wants to read, for learning, and for enjoyment.

DAVE'S PROGRESS IN WRITING

For help with Dave's writing and spelling, we have relied on the work of Diana Hanbury King.[8] Mrs. King, now a private educational consultant, founded and di-

Table 9. Dave's Errors on the WRAT Word Recognition Test

Word	Age 18	Age 22
form	*	from
grunt	glant	*
stretch	*	scratch
contagious	contanguous	*
grieve	greere	*
toughen	touchen	*
aboard	*	abroad
tranquillity	trangil	*
conspiracy	conspire	*
ethics	ethnic	ethnics
deny	deen	den
humiliate	humility	*
bibliography	bigblaography	bigliography
unanimous	anominous	anominous
predatory	predateor	perdictor
scald	scaled	scaled
mosaic	moisid	muscaic
municipal	munipal	*
decisive	deceive	deceive
deteriorate	deforick	*
stratagem	sterategem	stragatem
protuberance	*	protubulence
irascible	errscable	*
peculiarity	percul	perculitty
pugilist	plagist	*
enigmatic	emmatic	engimatic
covetousness	cotunnes	covetoreness
soliloquize	solquiz	soliquozzy
longevity	lontivity	*

*Word read correctly.

rected the Kildonan School in New York State and is nationally renowned for her work with dyslexics. It was Mrs. King who explained to me the special importance of teaching touch-typing to dyslexics. The point is not simply that they can then use a word processor with a spell-checker. Much more important, their fingers can be trained to spell automatically. That is, fingers can be trained to bypass the letter-sound correspondence disconnections and snarls that plague dyslexics.

For this to happen, the visual-motor letter patterns must become automated. As automaticity (Mrs. King calls it "motor memory") is established, the student's writing almost miraculously improves. At least Dave's did.

As Dave was practicing, I asked him to keep a log on his word processor of his experiences. I particularly emphasized that he was not to edit his log in any way. His first entry:

> On 2/27 I got to work with Diana King. The touch type listen [Dave's habitual way of spelling *lesson*] was very helpful in learning how to type. On my ability to type, I still have to partice more because I still have to look at the keys. The fash cards [an exercise of Mrs. King's] was deffent but was like some of the work we did in the lab. The writing [another exercise] was just a way to help orgizion your topics for each paragharphs. I do not know if this writing listen help. Writing is hard for me. I do not know if I just need to pratices more writing. Or build up my vocaluary so I can expense my ideas.

Dave kept to a strict practice schedule, using Mrs. King's workbook and other materials. He practiced at least ten hours a week. Three months later, his journal entries looked like this:

> It seemed that when I started going too fast, in spelling words in the spelling list with Rita [a college learning disabilities specialist] I started to switch letters like or to ro and, in the next word, I switched er to re. I also changed ou to uo in erroneous.
>
> I have to pay more attention when I do things because

if I do not things come out wrong or I should say switched.

I had a ten page paper to do in my business class. I had Rita go over it she said it was a good paper. So my writing may be improving but I still need more practice.

A week later, Dave burst into Rita's office with the news that he had received a 90 on his paper.

Dave will of course be practicing, as he puts it, for the rest of his life. He has a handicap that will never be completely overcome, and he will always make grateful use of technological aids and sympathetic friends. But by dint of hard work, and not giving way to frustration and discouragement, Dave has acquired the skills he needs in order to function effectively in the career of his choice.[9] He has grown from a shy, afflicted boy into an inspiring young man.[10]

7/ Research on Dyslexia

How can research help us understand Dave's reading disability? What was fundamentally wrong? To begin answering these questions, we need to consider how an information processing system reads. It starts by picking up print. It holds the print as a raw image in the "mind's eye" (buffer) for about a quarter of a second, during which time working memory deals with it. Working memory encodes portions of the buffered images (letters), and constructs a program that associates this "outside" information with "inside" information retrieved from long-term memory. The nature of the program will depend upon the task at hand.

Suppose the task is to read words the way eight-year-old Dave used to read them. His working memory program was apparently something like this:

- Look at the first two letters of the word.
- Search long-term memory for a word beginning with the same two letters.
- If a word is found, say it.
- If a word is not found, say you don't know.

If the task is to read words the way twenty-two-year-old Dave reads them after Intensive Literacy training, his working memory program is now quite different:

- Look at the entire word.
- Locate the boundary of the first syllable.
- Look at the letters in that first syllable.
- Search long-term memory for their sounds (phonograms), and maintain them in working memory.
- Locate the boundary of the next syllable and repeat the process.
- When finished with the last syllable, say all the sounds being held in working memory.
- Activate associated networks in long-term memory (meaning, syntax, and so on).

This is, of course, a much longer and more complicated program, especially when the procedures are first being learned. After extensive practice, the steps become automatic, and the program can be executed quickly and efficiently.

An information processing system spells by first picking up sounds (from the teacher's dictation, or from self-dictation), which are held briefly as raw aural patterns in the "mind's ear." Working memory encodes portions of these patterns and constructs a program associating this "outside" information with "inside" information retrieved from long-term memory. A program for a short, familiar word might be:

- Listen to the sound pattern.
- Retrieve the letters associated with that sound pattern.
- Retrieve the motor patterns for writing those letters down.

A program for a long, unfamiliar word might be:

- Listen to the sound pattern.
- Break it into syllables.
- Begin with the first syllable.

- Retrieve the letter(s) that represent the first sound.
- Write them down.
- Continue until the word is finished.

Although complete descriptions of working memory programs for reading and spelling would be very much more complicated, even these simple models are useful guides to the research literature on dyslexia. What might be going wrong? Is there evidence of defects in picking up and buffering printed letters or speech sounds? Is there evidence of defects at the working memory level? Is there evidence of storage or retrieval defects in long-term memory?

Before I present some of the research which addresses those questions, let me emphasize two points: First, if one mechanism—such as the mechanism for picking up speech sounds—is defective, then ensuing mental operations will also be affected to some degree. Hence, research has tried to locate precipitating defects which may have set in motion a train of additional defective or compensatory mental operations. The second point, closely related to the first, is that neurological defects which occur at an early age (even before birth) change the entire course of brain development. A unique brain grows up in response to the defect. It is therefore not correct to assume, for example, that the brain of a twelve-year-old handicapped child is functionally equivalent to that of a normal eight-year-old. Thus the precipitating defects, the underlying causes for which we are searching, may have occurred long before particular research data were collected.

SEEING THE PRINTED WORD

Dave looked at the word *deteriorate* and said "deforick." Is it possible he didn't see the printed word correctly? Answering that question is not a simple matter of giving Dave an eye test, or asking him to copy geometric patterns or to memorize Chinese ideograms. Dave's vision was normal and he could perform such tasks quite handily. But those tasks have no relationship to the special task of seeing print—black lines and curves of approximately the same dimensions, closely spaced, which must be picked up in sequences of eye movements. There are perceptual problems peculiar to seeing print, which can be understood only through the theory and technology of the field of vision research. This field studies the anatomical substrate of visual perception: specific cells on the retina, their dispersion and function, and their connections to cells deep within the brain that are activated by such stimuli as edges, color, amount of light, and so on. Much vision research is conducted on animals, since animals and humans share portions of their visual anatomy. Experimentation involves extremely precise control of visual stimuli, of their temporal duration (often only a few thousandths of a second will be critical), and of response measures.

The research summarized here was conducted in part by Bruno Breitmeyer at the University of Houston, and in part by William Lovegrove of the University of Tasmania in Hobart, Australia.[1]

BREITMEYER'S FORMULATION

When you move your eyes along a line of print you see a few words clearly in your focal vision. At the same time you see other words—above and below, left and right—in your peripheral vision. Bruno Breitmeyer has investigated the interrelated mechanisms underlying this perceptual experience.[2] One of his main discoveries is that there are two anatomically and functionally distinct mechanisms involved: a mechanism that operates during fixation, and a mechanism that operates during eye movements (saccades). These are known as sustained and transient mechanisms, respectively. They are composed of different kinds of visual cells which respond to different kinds of stimuli, as shown in Table 10.[3]

The sustained mechanism is active when you are looking directly at small graphic details for relatively long time periods. The transient mechanism is active during the short bursts of time when your eyes are in motion, and are being guided by large blocks of print in your peripheral vision. For example, transient cells pick up information about the length and shape of words in your right visual field. Most importantly, when one system (sustained or transient) turns on, it simultaneously turns off the other system. This type of mutual inhibition is widespread throughout the brain, and is essential to its efficient functioning.

Figure 18 shows the complementary on-off time periods of the two mechanisms.[4] The total time depicted is a little over one second. Shaded portions show how long a given mechanism is turned on—at most for about half a second.

The top line shows the duration of fixations and sac-

Table 10. Response Sensitivities of Sustained and Transient Brain Cells

Cell Characteristic	Sustained	Transient
Spatial frequency most sensitive to:	High (fine, narrow)	Low (coarse, wide)
Temporal frequency most sensitive to:	Slow	Fast
Period of response	Stimulus on	Stimulus turning on or off
Location	Central vision	Peripheral vision
When active, inhibits	Transient cells	Sustained cells

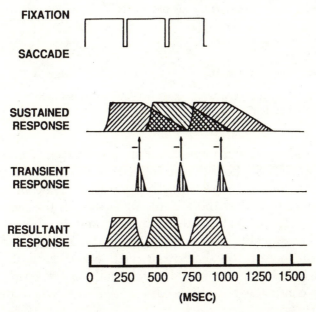

Figure 18. Duration of sustained and transient mechanisms.

cades. The horizontal portions of the line show three fixations and two intervening saccades. The next line shows onset, duration, and gradual decline of the sustained activation periods. Note the overlap (this is very important): while cells turned on by the first fixation are still active, new cells will be turned on by the next fixation. The third line shows the activation period of the transient mechanism. Each burst occurs when an eye movement (a saccade) is in progress. This crucial transient function turns off the sustaining operation of the previous fixation. Hence, the bottom line shows that each new fixation is uncluttered by remnants of the previous fixation.

Figure 19 illustrates the subjective experience of reading the phrase "Normal vision is iconoclastic."[5] If the

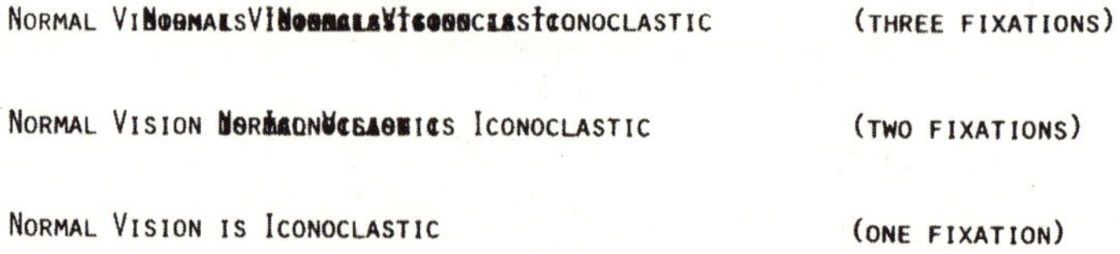

Normal Vi̇N̲o̲ğ̲ǎm̲ǎ̲l̲sVi̇N̲o̲ğ̲ǎm̲ǎ̲l̲a̲V̲i̲s̲o̲ğ̲ǎc̲l̲a̲s̲t̲c̲onoclastic　　　　　(THREE FIXATIONS)

Normal Vision N̲o̲r̲ǎ̲a̲o̲n̲V̲c̲b̲ǎ̲o̲ǎ̲i̲c̲s Iconoclastic　　　　　(TWO FIXATIONS)

Normal Vision is Iconoclastic　　　　　(ONE FIXATION)

Figure 19. What is seen when the transient mechanism fails to "clear the buffer."

phrase is read in a single fixation, it is clearly perceived, as shown in the bottom row. If two fixations are required, *and the transient mechanism fails,* portions of the phrase are experienced as the muddle illustrated in the second row. If three fixations are required, and the transient mechanism fails, the subjective muddle resembles the one in the top row. Failure or relative weakness of the transient mechanism may be what underlies the perceptual confusions experienced by dyslexics when they read.

The transient and sustained neural fibers extend from the retina, along the visual pathway, deep into the cortical and subcortical areas of the brain, where they interconnect with many other neurons. Damage to the transient or sustained mechanisms could occur deep within the brain, not in the eye, nor in the visual pathways that connect the eye to the brain.

This has special implications for development. A disorder in the growth of central portions of the brain could selectively impair either the sustained or transient mechanisms early in life. And, indeed, there is evidence from neurological research that dyslexics have in fact suffered microscopic damage to central brain tissue prior to birth. But the first question is which of the two mechanisms identified by Breitmeyer might be defective in dyslexics. For the answer, we turn to research by Lovegrove.

LOVEGROVE'S FORMULATION

The sustained and transient systems are affected by different factors and respond to stimuli in different ways. William Lovegrove and his colleagues capitalized upon these facts in order to compare the two systems in normal and dyslexic subjects.[6] In a series of experiments on normal and dyslexic children between the ages of five and fifteen, they found that normal and dyslexic children do not differ in the operations of the sustained mechanism, but they do differ in the operations of the transient mechanism. The saccadic suppression function is weaker in dyslexic children. That means that dyslexic children probably perceive the visual "overprinting" shown in Figure 19, periodically and unpredictably.

Lovegrove also addressed the question of whether these visual impairments were accompanied by auditory impairments. For some years researchers have been looking for discrete subtypes of dyslexia, usually a visual type on the one hand and a phonological type on the other. Lovegrove administered phonological tests to his dyslexic subjects and discovered that they were impaired in the phonological domain as well. It is likely that dyslexics have both visual and phonological difficulties, although a given individual may be more impaired in one area than in the other.

DETECTING AND HOLDING THE SOUNDS OF PRINT

Using written language—reading, writing, and spelling—means dealing with speech written down. When you write, you encipher speech in a graphic code. When you read, you decipher the writing back into speech.

Normally we are not aware of the involvement of speech, although sometimes we may spell or read out loud. The brain processes that underlie skilled reading and writing operate well below the level of consciousness and can be studied only by special technologies.

The Haskins Laboratories in New Haven, Connecticut, have been a fountainhead of research into speech, hearing, language, and related functions, including reading. The work of Isabelle Liberman, Alvin Liberman, and Donald Shankweiler is of special importance. Their most recent work has addressed the issue of exactly how language and reading are related—or rather, not related. The title of an article by Alvin Liberman says it well: "Reading Is Hard Just Because Listening Is Easy."[7]

To oversimplify a complex biological story, human anatomy has evolved over millions of years to process the expression and reception of speech in very efficient ways. We can produce and comprehend strings of consonants and vowels extremely rapidly because we overlap and merge speech sounds so that they are processed in parallel. Thus we speak and hear the word "bag" as a unified sound, not as a series of separately enunciated consonants and vowels. The term for this is "coarticulation."[8]

The fact that words are processed as wholes means that it is easy to learn graphic symbols for words as wholes. Written language started out several thousand years ago as systems of pictographs and logographs. But logographic languages turned out to be a tremendous burden on memory, as anyone who has studied Chinese can testify. Imagine having to learn a separate (if not completely unrelated) symbol for every word you know. Syllabaries are somewhat less taxing. Symbols for portions of words are mixed and matched, reducing some of the memory load. But far and away the most efficient writing systems are alphabetic, which is why the alphabetic principle has been discovered and rediscovered in many different linguistic cultures, and why it now characterizes almost every written language on the planet.[9] Alphabetic languages permit an infinite number of words to be generated from a very small set of letter-sound particles.

The problem with this principle, however, is that it requires users to break a holistically processed speech signal into its component parts. "Bag" has to be broken into a consonant-vowel-consonant sequence, so that the letters representing each component can be learned. This decomposition conflicts with the natural tendency to hear the word as a whole.

The ability to reflect upon a stream of speech sounds, and to detect those sound particles which are to be mapped onto letters, has been termed phonological awareness. Exactly what this ability involves physiologically is not fully understood, but it is clear that some people are natively endowed with more of it than others are, and that low phonological awareness underlies reading problems. It is also clear that the ability can be developed by training, especially before learning to read. Many recent studies have conclusively shown that children who receive phonological awareness training throughout kindergarten learn to read and spell much better than children who do not receive such training.[10]

Even among the most highly trained children, however, there will be a few—perhaps 10 or 15 percent of a class—who have difficulty. They find it very hard to reflect upon their own speech and to identify the sound particles (phonemes) that are represented by graphic particles (graphemes), as specified by alphabetic rules.

Dave (from Chapter 6) is one of those individuals. In addition to his visual difficulties with print, Dave has an

extremely hard time breaking words into their component sounds (segmentation), and putting those components together (blending). What underlies his problem?
Some answers have been provided by the research of
Joseph Torgesen, of Florida State University.

TORGESEN'S FORMULATION

Joseph Torgesen did not set out to investigate dyslexia.
He set out to investigate a subset of learning-disabled
children who differed from other learning-disabled children. Unexpectedly, he ended up discovering a mechanism that is associated with extreme inability to learn to
read.[11]

Torgesen was initially struck by the fact that some
learning-disabled children—as his local public schools
classified them—had exceptionally low scores on digit
span tests. Dave displayed a similar defect. When he was
eight years old, Dave had difficulty repeating sets of
numbers. Dave's examiner at that time noted, to his own
surprise, that Dave had no difficulty repeating meaningful sentences.

Torgesen conducted a series of investigations into the
precise nature of such a difficulty and its implications for
schoolwork. He found, to begin with, that learning-disabled children with low digit span did not perform
poorly on all short-term memory tests. This finding is
shown in Figure 20.[12] The filled circles show the performance of learning-disabled children with low digit span
(LD-S). The open circles show the performance of learning-disabled children with normal digit span (LD-N),
and the triangles show the performance of the normal
control group (N). There are no differences to speak of
among the groups on the Visual Sequential Memory and
Sorting-Recall tests. On the tests of Recognition Memory
and Memory for Content, both learning-disabled groups

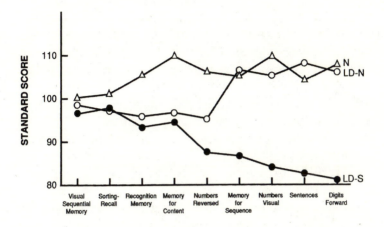

Figure 20. Performance by three groups of children on nine memory tasks. N = children of normal academic achievement; LD-N = learning-disabled children who performed in the average range on short-term memory tests; LD-S = learning-disabled children who performed poorly on short-term memory tests.

drop below the nondisabled children. On the Numbers Reversed test, the two learning-disabled groups diverge, and on the remaining tests the children with low digit span are far below the two other groups. As Torgesen summarized these findings:

> The performance of [learning-disabled children with low digit span] was impaired only on tasks that specifically required the immediate verbatim recall of sequences of verbal items. On these latter tasks, it did not matter whether the items were presented visually or embedded in meaningful sentences. . . . In contrast, they do not show impairments on tasks requiring the immediate recall of abstract (unfamiliar) visual information, on tasks that allow semantic [meaningful] encoding of items, or on recognition memory tasks.

In additional experiments, Torgesen probed for an explanation of this selective memory impairment. He ruled out a number of possibilities: motivation or attention was not the problem; the perception of temporal order was not the problem (we would know that in Dave's case, since he excelled in leading a drum corps); and strategy (such as rehearsing) was not the problem. On the basis of additional experiments, Torgesen concluded that the performance problems of low span children were caused by "difficulties utilizing verbal/phonological codes to store information."

We can think of this as a defect in the interaction of working memory with a buffer that is specialized for speech sounds. At this stage of processing, speech sounds are meaningless, since meaning has not yet been activated in long-term memory. The impairment that Torgesen's experiments isolated was the ability to hold and manipulate meaningless speech sounds in working memory—exactly the same ability that Liberman and her colleagues called phonological awareness.

Torgesen then examined the difficulties that his low digit span children were having in school, and found that they were severely deficient in reading. Further, he found on follow-up tests that, unlike the other two groups, the low span group showed almost no improvement in reading skills over a nine-year period.[13] Their test scores looked very much like Dave's scores in Table 5. Thus, although Torgesen had not started out to do so, he isolated a crucial characteristic of a group of children who probably should have been classified as dyslexic.[14]

TYPES OF DYSLEXIA

Normal readers can deal with print in diversified ways. We saw four sample working memory programs at the beginning of this chapter. Sometimes a normal reader picks up and buffers visual word cues, and encodes them as visual symbols in working memory; these visual symbols, in turn, activate meaning networks in long-term memory. This is what you do when you "read by sight." Alternatively, sometimes a normal reader translates visual cues into sounds, by referring to alphabetic letter-sound rules (which may or may not be the correct rules, incidentally); these sound symbols then activate meaning networks in long-term memory. This is what you do when you "sound out" a word, especially an unfamiliar word.

These two modes of reading involve different neurological pathways. In persons who suffer brain injury after they have learned to read, one pathway, and one type of reading, may be impaired, but not the other. In some cases of brain injury, the patient loses the ability to sound out words. The letter-sound "rule box" seems to have been deleted from the patient's brain. (The patient can, however, recognize familiar words visually.) This is called phonological dyslexia. In other cases of brain injury, the patient loses the ability to recognize even highly frequent words visually, although the patient can apply letter-sound rules. Thus, such a patient would pronounce the word *have* to rhyme with *save*. That type of acquired disorder is technically called surface dyslexia, but for simplicity we can think of it as visual dyslexia.[15]

There are many more modes of normal reading than the two we have mentioned (sight reading and sounding out). You can read aloud, read silently, point to words, sing words, spell words aloud, emphasize words in your mind, skim, puzzle over the meaning of a word or a phrase, search text for a particular name, and so on. All of these different ways of reading involve different neurological patterns, and for almost every pattern you can think of, a patient has been found somewhere in whom that pattern has been disrupted by injury. For each such patient, a new type of dyslexia has been described.[16]

There are peripheral dyslexias and central dyslexias. There is neglect dyslexia, attentional dyslexia, letter-by-letter dyslexia, reading without meaning (sometimes called "hyperlexia" in very young or retarded children who can read words but don't know what they mean), semantic access dyslexia, and deep dyslexia (sometimes thought to be reading with the right hemisphere instead of with the left, where the language area is usually located).

Similarly, many types of writing and spelling disorders have been identified in patients who lost the ability to write and spell as a result of brain trauma. There are patients who have lost the ability to speak (traumatic aphasia), even to use inner speech, but who retain the ability to write. This is called phonological dysgraphia. In deep dysgraphia, patients write "moon" when *star* has been dictated, or "time" when *hour* was dictated. There is a type of dysgraphia called word meaning deafness, and a type called surface dysgraphia. There is peripheral dysgraphia, central dysgraphia, graphic motor pattern dysgraphia, and afferent dysgraphia.

To make the picture even more complicated, a close reading of each case history reveals that patients don't always display the expected symptoms. Some words elicit the symptoms; other words don't. The complex in each case is far from clear. Nevertheless, such diversity in cases of acquired dyslexia would lead us to predict diversity in cases of developmental dyslexia as well. Many attempts have been made to classify developmental dyslexics into subtypes similar to those found in acquired dyslexics, but the results are just as confusing. New research is therefore moving in a different direction.

PRENATAL BRAIN INJURY

The only way to know for sure if developmental dyslexia has resulted from neurological defects is to examine the brains of dyslexics. The examination must be very fine-grained: thin slices of brain tissue must be studied microscopically. Such research obviously cannot be conducted on living brains. But through the auspices of The Orton Society, brains of deceased individuals who suffered from dyslexia are being contributed to the Dyslexia Neuroanatomical Laboratory at the Harvard Medical School. The research originated with the late Norman Geschwind, and is now under the direction of Albert Galaburda.[17]

Examination of ten brains of male and female dyslexics (mostly male) revealed several types of anomalies: clumps of immature neurons (brain cells) near the brain's surface (ectopias); neurons arranged irregularly instead of in regular layers (dysplasias); tiny enfoldings inside the brain that shouldn't be there (micropolygyria); tiny congenital tumors (oligodendrogliomas); and scars which may have blocked blood vessels (fibromyelin plaques). These anomalies are numerous (from 30 to 140 per dyslexic brain) and are most often localized in the left hemisphere. In a control series of ten nondyslexic brains, anomalies appeared only in three of the brains, and only one or two anomalies per nondyslexic brain.

It is known that such anomalies arise from "errors" during particular phases of prenatal brain growth. For example, between the eighteenth and twenty-fourth week of gestation, certain brain cells are manufactured in a lower area of the brain and then migrate to other areas, where they line up in regular arrays and "sprout." Some of the errors in dyslexic brains result from misplacement of these neurons. The migrating cells lodge and sprout in the wrong places, functioning there like small nonconducting scars. Such errors can arise from many possible sources. In the case of dyslexia, they are probably caused by factors associated with autoimmunological disorders: asthma, allergies, diabetes, rheumatoid arthritis, and so on—disorders in the body's ability to protect itself against its own products. These disorders are often associated with dyslexia, and both kinds of disorders run in the same families.[18] There is a possibility that substances manufactured in connection with autoimmunological disorders cause the tiny fetal brain injuries that result in dyslexia. Animal studies have supported that conjecture.[19]

Once these early forms of damage have occurred, however, the growing brain begins to compensate for them. The brain "rewires" itself around dysfunctional areas and increases the number of neurons in other areas. In particular, early damage in the left hemisphere spurs compensatory growth of the right hemisphere. Normally the left hemisphere is larger and heavier than the right, but the brains of dyslexics are symmetrical. The right hemisphere has generated more neurons than it should have. These symmetrical brains also have a greater number of callosal fibers, which connect the left and right hemispheres.

This has interesting implications for Orton's theory of dyslexia (described in Chapter 2). Orton believed that the right hemisphere "intruded" into operations that were normally controlled by the left hemisphere. The left hemisphere was unable to suppress the intrusions. The results included distortions in speech and writing and interference in visual-sound associations and sound-meaning associations. The research that Galaburda and Geschwind conducted, using technology that was not available in Orton's time, showed that the anatomy of dyslexic brains was consistent with Orton's theory: the right hemisphere has more power than it ought to have.[20]

Not all the effects of a "superdeveloped" right hemisphere are necessarily bad. We should anticipate that many dyslexics will display unusual abilities of the right hemispheric type: pattern-processing, holistic, visualizing capabilities. Dave's skills as a drum major—his ability to deal simultaneously with interlocking melodic, rhythmic, visual, and motion patterns, provides one example. The case of a dyslexic girl who was talented in art is described in Chapter 9.

Bear in mind, however, that a superdeveloped right hemisphere is not the *cause* of dyslexia. Anomalous brain structures are not in themselves handicapping. Where a handicap is associated with an unusual structure, then both the handicap and the unusual structure have been caused by some underlying pathology. In the case of dyslexia, Galaburda's research has shown what that underlying pathology is, and how it could precipitate both a superdeveloped right hemisphere and the handicap of dyslexia.

This research also helps explain why it has been so difficult to classify developmental dyslexics into a few distinct subtypes. In each individual case, the nature and location of the tiny zones of brain damage are different. The responses of the growing brain to the injuries are different. The ways the brain copes with diversified reading and spelling tasks are different. And numerous other factors also vary—personality, family circumstances, intelligence, educational opportunity, and cultural background.

Galaburda's most recent research has focused on the cellular architecture of two visual systems: the magnocellular pathway and the parvocellular pathway, which are distinguished, in part, by the properties listed in Table 10.[21] The magnocellular system is the anatomical basis for what Breitmeyer calls the transient mechanism. Both types of cells (magno and parvo) are most easily distinguished in a part of the brain known as the lateral geniculate nucleus, or LGN.

Galaburda microscopically examined sections of the LGN in a sample of brains of dyslexic and nondyslexic persons. He found that the magnocellular layers were more disorganized in the dyslexic's brains, and the cell bodies appeared smaller, which means they were probably, in effect, "sluggish." That could account for the fact that in dyslexia, the magno (transient) system doesn't do an effective job of wiping the visual slate clean. The type of perceptual confusion shown in Figure 19 might well result.

All told, the domain of dyslexia research is narrowing fast. Over the next few years, findings from many different scientific fields should converge to explain, finally, a complex phenomenon that has fascinated researchers for over a hundred years. With the ultimate explanation will come new methods of remedial instruction.

8/ Spatial and Mathematical Disabilities

CONSTRUCTIONAL DYSPRAXIA

The handwriting in Figure 21 is by a college student who has an IQ in the Very Superior range, and SATs of more than 1400. He has no problems with spelling or syntax; he is not dyslexic. But he consistently fails to space words and sentences. It's as if the "space bar" is missing from his handwriting control system.

Figure 22 shows the work of an eight-year-old boy. His teacher had asked her third graders to copy four arithmetic problems from the blackboard. Bobby, an above-average reader, could not copy them correctly.

Figure 23 shows the attempt of a college student to copy a set of simple patterns.

These kinds of spatial difficulties can be distinguished from dysgraphia, the spelling and writing disorder that often accompanies dyslexia (see Figure 17). They can also be distinguished from motor-control problems (ataxia) such as those found in cerebral palsy. Pure difficulty with drawing, and sometimes also with the arrangement of objects, is termed "constructional dyspraxia" by neuropsychologists. The term means "disorder of movements under visual control, particularly affecting the spatial components of the task."[1]

129

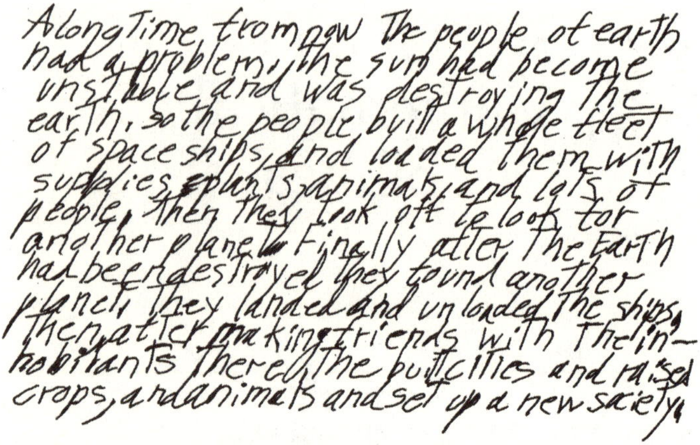

A long Time from now The people of earth had a problem, the sun had become unstable and was destroying The earth, so the people built a whole fleet of space ships, and loaded them with supplies, plants, animals, and lots of people, then they took off to look for another planet. Finally after The Earth had been destroyed they found another planet, they landed and unloaded The ships, Then, after making friends with The inhobitants There, The built cities and raised crops, and animals and set up a new society.

Figure 21. Spacing problems in handwriting of a college student.

On the blackboard:

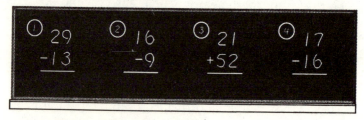

As Bobby copied them:

Figure 22. Copying problems of a third-grade student.

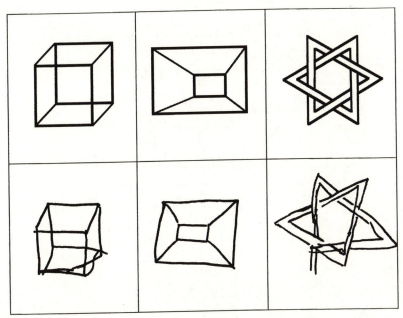

Figure 23. Copying problems of a college student.

DRAWING SUBROUTINES

Drawing, like reading and spelling, is a complex task. Goals must be set, cues must be picked up visually, knowledge must be retrieved, feedback must be processed, and so on. An extensive analysis of the many cognitive factors involved has been conducted by Peter van Sommers of Macquarie University in Australia.[2]

Van Sommers identified a number of drawing subroutines, some of which are shown in Figure 24. Each of these modules contains a myriad of processes. Analysis, recognition, and meaning initiate the drawing. The remaining subroutines are activated as the drawing is produced. Some of the procedures in the depiction decision module are shown in Figure 25. If I am going to draw a

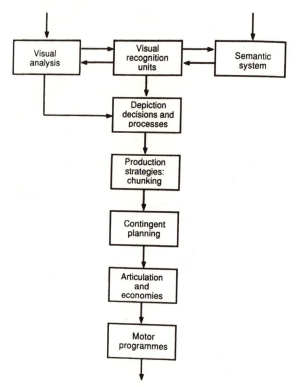

Figure 24. Drawing subroutines as schematized by Peter van Sommers.

tree, what kind of tree will it be? What will be my view of it? And so on.

The next subroutine is "chunking," assembling the parts of a figure or a scene that we perceive as units. For example, normally we see a window as a unit, not as a collection of vertical and horizontal lines. The next two modules—contingent planning, and articulation and economies—involve the application of general and specific drawing rules that people spontaneously construct. To draw a circle, the vast majority of people will start at the top and draw counterclockwise. To draw a sun, al-

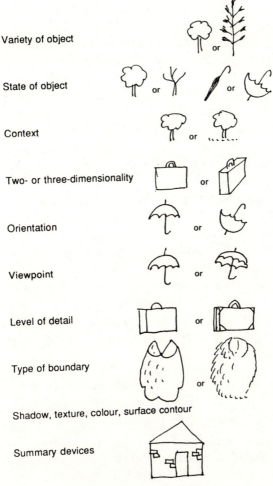

Variety of object

State of object

Context

Two- or three-dimensionality

Orientation

Viewpoint

Level of detail

Type of boundary

Shadow, texture, colour, surface contour

Summary devices

Figure 25. Depiction decisions.

most every child will draw the disc first, and then the rays that extend from it. Van Sommers has extensively documented these informal rules.[3] The final subroutine is the execution of hand movements.

Although diagrammed as a series, the subroutines interact, and often operate in parallel. It is therefore difficult to pinpoint exactly what has been impaired in cases of constructional dyspraxia. Van Sommers studied in depth the case of an architectural draftsman he called L.B., who suffered a stroke that damaged his right hemisphere in the vicinity of the cerebral artery.[4] L.B. lost the ability to draw patterns like the one shown in Figure 26 (A). The pattern was displayed for five seconds and L.B. then drew it from memory. This was repeated many times, and some of L.B.'s successive attempts to reproduce the pattern are shown in B through H.

By means of various tests, van Sommers concluded that L.B. had lost the ability to connect imaging processes to drawing strategies. The difficulty, in other words, was localized in the module of depiction decisions. You can get a feeling for this by reflecting upon your own strategies for drawing this figure from memory. You will probably encode the figure as a cloverleaf movement pattern. L.B. encoded only fragments of the visual pattern, and was unable to connect them to movement patterns.

DYSPRAXIC DISORDERS AND BASIC ACADEMIC SKILLS

L.B.'s handicap clearly impaired his ability to perform his job as a draftsman. But did it impair his ability to speak, read, write, and calculate? L.B.'s stroke, remember, damaged a portion of his right hemisphere. We would therefore predict that his speech, which is normally localized in the left hemisphere, would be unimpaired. That proved to be correct. But his reading, writing, spelling, and calculation did not escape damage. These skills are not performed solely by the left hemisphere. The pattern processing, spatial abilities of the right hemisphere may also play important roles.

A recent Harvard Medical School report confirmed this. When forty consecutive patients admitted with

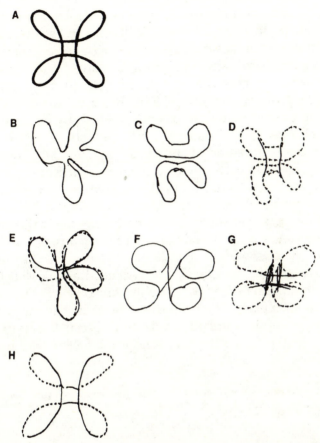

Figure 26. Successive attempts by L.B. to copy a design (A). Solid lines show what he drew first; dotted lines, what he added later.

right-hemispheric damage were given a battery of tests, it was found that verbal impairments accompanied visual and spatial impairments in most cases. The more severe the spatial impairments, the more severe the verbal deficits—for example, in the ability to summarize a narrative.[5]

Nevertheless, it is possible for impairments in drawing

and spatial-construction skills to be independent of impairments in basic academic skills. The most dramatic examples are cases of idiot-savant artists or calculators, severely retarded individuals who display outstanding talents in drawing or arithmetic. Two British researchers, Neil O'Connor and Beate Hermelin, used some of van Sommers' test materials to compare the drawing abilities of eleven-year-old normal children and twenty-two-year-old retarded adults (with IQs of about 50).[6] Half of the subjects in each group were talented artistically, and half were not. Examples of their drawings, which were rated on a scale of 1 to 5, are shown in Figure 27.

Drawings that showed constructional dyspraxia were produced only by the nontalented retarded persons. The idiot savants, who were quite unable to succeed in regular academic programs, showed no drawing deficits. On the contrary, they were highly skilled (see Figure 28).

Another example of the disconnection that can exist between basic academic skills and special talents was seen in the film *Rain Man*. The actor Dustin Hoffman

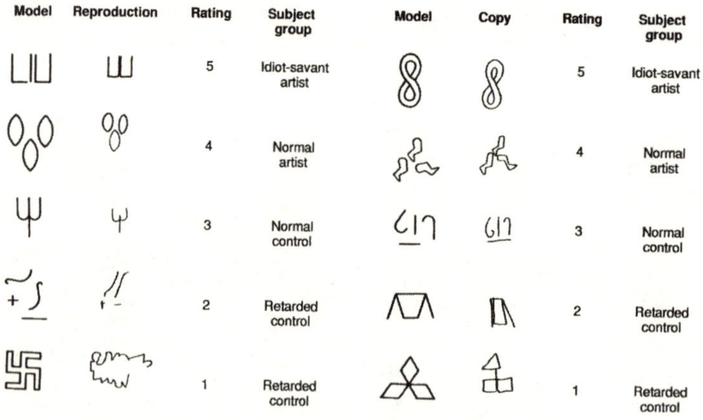

Figure 27. Examples of drawings and ratings.

very accurately depicted a man suffering from Asperger's Syndrome. The film didn't reveal the character's abilities on tests that measure constructional dyspraxia—such as puzzles and matching block designs—or his drawing abilities, but Asperger's patients tend to be relatively good on such tests, even if they don't display the extraordinary talents shown in Figure 28. The film did show that the character had remarkable counting abilities (during his card-counting adventure in Las Vegas). Yet he had no grasp of the logic of simple arithmetic (as shown in the scene in the doctor's office).

All this suggests that although there may be connections between spatial abilities (or disabilities) and arithmetic abilities (or disabilities), the connections are not simple ones. To explain, let us look more closely at what arithmetic disabilities involve.

Figure 28. Sketch by an idiot savant with an IQ of 50.

DYSCALCULIA

The phenomenon called dyscalculia is broadly defined as an inability to perform the operations of arithmetic. This is not a simple matter of forgetting a few numbers or rules, but we are far from knowing exactly what the problems are. Most of what we can say about arithmetic disorders comes from the study of brain-damaged adults, people who have suffered bullet wounds or tumors. It is not yet clear—as it seems to be in the case of dyslexia—that an analogous type of brain dysfunction might be inborn in children who cannot learn arithmetic.

If there is such a thing as developmental dyscalculia, and if our knowledge of it must be shaped by our knowledge of traumatic adult dyscalculia, then what kinds of behavior should we be looking for?

THE LOSS OF MATHEMATICAL SKILLS IN ADULTS

A. R. Luria's general theory of brain function was briefly presented in Chapter 5. Essentially Luria believed that specific parts of the brain were responsible for specific parts of tasks. Imagery, for example, was thought to be a function of the occipital lobes in the back of the head. Any task that has an imagery component, then, would be disrupted by damage to the occipital areas. Luria's work makes us conscious of the many phenomena of arithmetic disability, and of the subtle and complex forms that errors may take. Luria studied four types of arithmetic disorders.[7]

Type I: Defects of logic. Logical defects are revealed by a patient's inability to understand phrases like "a triangle below a cross." If such a phrase were dictated, the patient might write (or draw) the elements in the order they were named, without regard to relationships among the elements. Note that the relationships have a spatial aspect. To grasp them, one must hold the elements in mind simultaneously and compare them in some dimension.

Logical defects can also appear in the handling of numbers. For example, a patient might write the number 1029 as 129, thus demonstrating a failure to grasp the logic of zero as a place-holder. Similarly, the patient might write the number as 1000 29—in the order the numbers were named, without regard to the relationships signified.

Logical defects of this type probably have their origin in spatial problems. Apparently what has been lost is the ability to maintain spatial reference points, such as the location of the tens, the ones, and so forth. "The analysis of compound numbers formed in accordance with the decimal system requires the differentiation of categories occupying different positions in space when written, and even when imagined they retain their spatial organization. It is clear, therefore, that when spatial syntheses are disturbed and . . . spatial ideas have disintegrated, the categorical structure of number is fundamentally upset."[8] Such patients also have difficulty understanding calendars and clocks.

The writing and drawing in Figure 29 was produced by a twenty-four-year-old naval officer a few weeks before an operation for a brain cyst in the right frontal region, the same region Luria described as affecting spatial logic. We can see from the patient's writing that he had difficulty orienting letters in words. He could not produce the digits 389×68 to dictation. When told that $8 \times 9 = 72$, he was not able to place the 72 properly. At the top right is his attempted drawing of a man. The materials below were produced two days later. The abil-

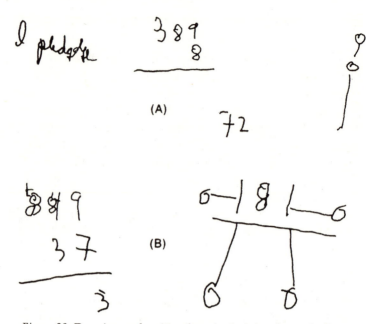

Figure 29. Drawing and writing by a brain-injured naval officer.

ity to form the digits had deteriorated, and he could not complete the operations of multiplication. His ability to draw a figure was even more distorted.[9]

Type II: Defects in planning. Luria described an adult patient who was given this problem: "A boy is eight years old. His father is thirty years older, and his mother is ten years younger than the father. How old are they?"[10] The patient began to solve the problem in the following way: "Each part here must have thirty and then ten and then eight, that makes forty-eight and divide by three." The problem was repeated, and the patient realized that she had replied incorrectly: "I should have said the son was eight years old and the father thirty years older. I gave the wrong answer. I should have said the father was thirty eight years old and the mother, uh, the mother was twenty years old." The problem was explained to her again, and she began to solve it correctly, although when she said "The father is thirty years older and the mother ten years younger," again she impulsively subtracted ten from thirty and concluded that the mother was twenty years old. Finally, the fourth time around, she got the problem right.

Luria said this patient and others like her regularly failed to perform a preliminary analysis of the conditions of the problem. As a result, the patient was never able to formulate a plan for solving the problem. Instead, the patient jumped into impulsive arithmetic operations and lost all connection with the original problem. Luria said she also regularly failed to verify her answers. Once she got some kind of answer, she was willing to settle for it. (Since this particular defect sounds very much like ordinary carelessness, it is most interesting to learn that it cleared up following the removal of a brain tumor.)

Type III: Perseveration of procedures that are no longer appropriate. Luria frequently tested patients on tasks of the following type: "On two shelves were eighteen books, but not equally divided. On one shelf there were twice as many as on the other. How many books were there on each shelf?" The protocol of a patient attempting to solve that problem, along with Luria's comments on the protocol, are reproduced below.[11]

Protocol
The patient begins to solve the problem thus: "On two shelves there were eighteen books . . . on one there were twice . . . no, that won't work . . . if they were equally divided there would have been nine." But there were twice as many on one shelf. "On one nine . . . no, then they would be equal . . . nine divided by two is four and

one-half, that means four and one-half and twelve and one-half.

"No . . . on one, four, and on the second, fourteen." . . . Why four? "Well, if it can't be four and one-half, then it must be four. The half is impossible. Had it been 20, I would have subtracted."

Comments

The patient cannot reject the number nine, and in subsequent calculations he is guided by it, continuing to divide the number obtained by half. Solution of the problem is replaced by the formal rejection of a fractional part of the number.

Luria then explained the principle of what he termed "sharing into parts" to the patient, who understood the principle and could apply it to new problems of the same form. However, when the form of the problem was changed, the patient crashed on the shoals of the new rule. "On two shelves there were eighteen books, but there were two books fewer on one shelf than on the other. How many books were there on each shelf?"

Protocol

"That means, two books fewer . . . perhaps nine and seven." How did you solve it? "Eighteen shared by two is nine, and then two fewer." Is that right? "Sixteen . . . No, there are eighteen in the problem . . . These must also be shared . . . by two . . . they must be taken away . . . Eighteen by two . . . there were two fewer on one shelf . . . we must divide into three parts . . . On one shelf there were twelve and on the others six . . . Eighteen altogether." Is that right? "No . . . there were two fewer!" (Gives up.)

Comments

The old method of dividing into halves springs out at first, followed by the [new] method of sharing into parts

[but] into the same number of parts dictated by the previous problem.

In the defects described thus far, the patients showed disabled organizational or procedural functions. They could calculate quite well. Precisely the opposite difficulty was shown by a patient with the fourth type of dyscalculia.

Type IV: Inability to perform simple calculations. This particular patient had been an artillery commander and had previously demonstrated a high degree of skill in performing gun-placement calculations. As a result of a bullet wound, the patient lost the ability to perform simple calculations, but maintained the ability to analyze problems and even to invent new strategies for circumventing his calculation defect. After his injury, the patient understood the logic of number and could still count forward and backward, even by twos or fives. However, he would have to go through the entire series from the beginning before he could produce the next number in the series. At first, the patient also appeared able to add normally, though slowly. But more careful analysis revealed that the patient was adding by counting. To add seventeen and twenty, for example, he would start with seventeen and count on for twenty counts. He kept track of his counts on his fingers. The patient had no memories of addition facts or of multiplication facts—he multiplied by counting as well. "If they say: multiply 3 × 4, previously I would have replied immediately, but now I cannot do it, there are simply 3 and 4. I know that I should multiply, but all I can do is take it to pieces and add—3, and 3 again, and the same again a second time."[12]

The patient clearly understood the logic of multiplication, but the tables themselves had been wiped out of his memory. Nor was he able to relearn them very successfully. After a month of practice, he had learned the tables only up to five, and they were still not automatic. When asked to multiply three times two he would work it out by counting. When Luria stopped the patient from counting by having him hold the tip of his tongue between his teeth, the patient became totally unable to calculate. "I can't do it at all, my tongue is held, and I cannot speak, everything is spinning round." The patient eventually became able to calculate with groups of five. "I can see that five is the same as five fingers, and these are all ready for use in calculation." He even developed a method of performing division by counting fives. "Twenty-eight divided by four . . . (thinks for a long time) makes seven. This is how I did it: I added the four groups of five, and got twenty, which left eight. Two will go into this four times; five and two make seven."[13] The patient was also helped by his memory of other highly familiar groups. For example, in the army he had called up his men three times a day, and a line of men was ten. Hence, the number eight could be recalled as "two missing from a line of ten men." Although the patient gradually improved with practice, the old calculation fluency never returned.

What exactly was the nature of this defect? It was not simply a loss of number memory because the patient was able to retrieve any number by counting up to it. But counting seemed to be the only number-manipulation scheme available to him. By schemes, Luria meant highly automated calculation habits into which numbers could fit. The patient did not lose the numbers; he lost the schemes to put them in.

FAILURE OF MATHEMATICAL SKILLS IN CHILDREN

It is instructive to compare Luria's cases with some described by Herbert Ginsburg in his analysis of children's difficulties in learning arithmetic. These are children who have no known form of brain damage.

Ginsburg is a psychologist who has specialized in the study of children's natural strategies for quantifying their world and for coping with formal mathematical instruction. His book, *Children's Arithmetic*, offers many illustrations of children's spontaneous arithmetic thinking. One of Ginsburg's cases fits in with Type I, logical defects that may have a spatial component.

> Ralph, an eleven-year-old fifth grader working about two years below grade level, showed a . . . gap between written work and informal knowledge [of arithmetic]. Indeed, his informal skills were impressive. Given collections of objects to add (for example, 23 pennies and 18 pennies), he would group the objects and count by fives or tens. He solved mental problems by clever regrouping strategies. For example, to add 75 + 58, "I took the 70 and 50, counted by tens and that made 120. Then I took the 5 from the 75 and that made 125. From the 8, I took 5 more for 130 and 3 more is 133." He was also adept at subtraction involving real objects and mental subtraction; in both cases he used grouping or regrouping strategies.
>
> At the same time, Ralph's written computations were seriously in error. He lined up numbers from left to right, as in
>
> $$\begin{array}{r} 23 \\ +\ 5 \\ \hline 73 \end{array}$$
>
> He did not know how to carry. For example, given
>
> $$\begin{array}{r} 19 \\ +\ 16 \end{array}$$
>
> he began to add from the left, doing 1 + 1 = 2. Next he did 9 + 6 = 15, which would have given
>
> $$\begin{array}{r} 19 \\ +\ 16 \\ \hline 215 \end{array}$$

But somehow he realized that 215 contained too many digits. His solution was simply to ignore the 5 in 215! This yielded an answer of 21. In the case of subtraction, he was asked to do 15 − 7 on paper (he had already obtained the correct answer in his head) and wrote

$$\begin{array}{r} 15 \\ -\,7 \\ \hline 65 \end{array}$$

After having lined up the numbers incorrectly, he used the common method of subtracting the smaller number from the larger.

We see then that Ralph was skilled at arithmetic except when he had to do it on paper . . . Ralph would never work problems on paper, unless I told him to do so. And wildly contradictory answers didn't bother Ralph in the least. He seemed to believe that one gets different answers when problems are worked out on paper, rather than in an informal way [mentally], and that both procedures are correct. When I asked Ralph which answer is right, he said "Both." And when I asked why, he said "It's different." For Ralph, written work and informal procedures are separate, but equal.[14]

If Luria were to analyze Ralph's behavior, he would probably say that different parts of the brain were involved in the informal and written procedures; that the written procedures invoked spatial brain functions, while the informal procedures invoked motor functions (physical grouping) and verbal functions (counting). Informal procedures can, of course, involve spatial processes, but with Ralph they probably did not. The case illustrates the very important fact that arithmetic logic, or the absence of it, can depend on the way the information is represented mentally. If Ralph were required to use a spatial representation, he appeared very illogical. If he were permitted to use an alternative representation, he appeared logical and clever.

But not all children are so efficient at switching from one representational strategy to another. Another of Ginsburg's cases illustrates Type III, perseveration of inappropriate procedures.

Patty was asked to write down the sum of 10 + 1. She wrote:

$$\begin{array}{r} 10 \\ + 1 \\ \hline 20 \end{array}$$

In an attempt to help Patty see what was wrong, the interviewer (I) said:

I: Well, suppose you couldn't use paper at all, and I said how much is 10 plus 1?
P: I'd count on my fingers.
I: Why don't you do it?
Patty held up all ten fingers and stared at them.
P: You have 10 (she looked at the fingers). You put the zero on the bottom (draws a zero with her finger).
I: Just use your fingers now.
P: Then you put 2 and you add 1 and 1 and it's 2.
Patty seemed unable to count 10 on her fingers! Instead she persisted in using the written procedure, apparently doing [it] in her head . . .
I: What about on your fingers? Show me how you do it on your fingers. You can use my fingers too. Put out your fingers too.
P: You put the zero on.
I: No, I don't see any zeros. All I see are these little fingers. Never mind zeros.
P: That's hard. (She looked as though thinking intently.)
I: Now you have all kinds of fingers to work with, Patty. Now you figure out how much is 10 plus 1.
P: You have to put a zero underneath.
I: I don't see any zero at all. All I see are these fingers.
P: O.k. If you want zero you have to take these ten away (she pointed to the interviewer's fingers). You put zero,

then you have 1 and 1 left and you add them up and you get 20. So it's 20.
I: Can you do it without zeros?
P: No.

Finally Ginsburg made an important discovery about Patty. The use of the word "plus" was locking Patty into the inappropriate procedure. If the wording of the problem were changed to "How many are 10 and 1 altogether?" Patty would promptly answer "eleven."

> Given the word *plus*, she applied an incorrect addition method to both objects and written numbers. Given *altogether* she used a sensible counting procedure, again for both object and written numbers. *Altogether* is a natural word for addition. Patty probably used it in everyday life to talk about adding things. *Plus* is a school word that Patty seems to have associated with a wrong algorithm that she did not understand.[15]

Again, Luria would probably suggest that different parts of the brain are activated by the use of different verbal association networks. Changing a word may change a whole network of brain connections.

IMPLICATIONS FOR DEVELOPMENTAL DYSCALCULIA

What do these examples of acquired dyscalculia and of faulty mathematical thinking in normal children imply about the nature of developmental dyscalculia? Each case is characterized by difficulties in coordinating verbal and spatial ideas. These difficulties apparently enter into failures of logic, failures of computation, and failures of place-keeping.

Support for this hypothesis is found in the research of Beate Hermelin and Neil O'Connor on children gifted in mathematics.[16] These children showed superior abilities in coordinating verbal and spatial ideas. The children in the study were about thirteen years old. They were compared to children of the same age and IQ who had average mathematical abilities, and also to children who were gifted in art. They were compared on two tests: one that measured visual memory, and one that measured skills in coordinating verbal and spatial representations. In the first test, the children reconstructed from memory patterns like those shown in Figure 30. On this task, the mathematically and artistically gifted children performed equally well, both better than the controls.

The coordination test was composed of questions like these: How many diagonals are there on the surface of a cube? If the hands of a clock are at right angles to each other and the hour hand points to twelve, what two times are possible? To answer such questions, the children had to hold in mind both the verbal queries and the visual images, and relate them. On this test, the mathematically gifted children were superior to the artistically gifted children, as well as to the controls:

Verbally presented tasks requiring spatial reasoning and the mental manipulation of spatial images, were better solved by the mathematically gifted than by either an IQ-matched control group, or by those gifted for the visual arts. . . . Those who are gifted for mathematics can convert verbal codes into spatial images, are able to operate on these images, and can then retranslate their solution into verbal form.[17]

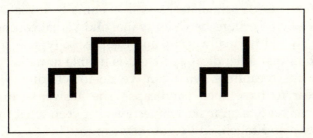

Figure 30. Example of materials used in pattern-memory test.

It follows that those who are disabled in mathematics may be impaired in those very same skills.

IMPLICATIONS FOR RESEARCH AND PRACTICE

I predict that research into the nature of spatial and mathematical disabilities will constitute the next major focus of the field of learning disabilities. This does not mean that research into the nature of dyslexia and dysgraphia will vanish; many problems remain to be investigated. But our understanding of spatial and mathematical disabilities runs well behind our understanding of reading, writing, and spelling disabilities, and the time has come to begin catching up.

What will characterize this burgeoning research, I hope, will be a sophisticated awareness of the complexity of school tasks that involve spatial and mathematical skills. For one thing, such tasks cannot be categorized simplistically as "nonverbal."[18] Geometry, for example, incorporates not only spatial figures but also verbal theorems. Geography involves the ability to imagine and to draw spatial forms, but it also requires learning verbal information such as place names. Even the ability to perform arithmetic calculations is partly a matter of verbally memorizing tables, and partly a matter of "seeing" patterns. Research into the information processing requirements of school tasks will eventually reveal the flow of connections between spatial and verbal concepts that should normally occur, and the precise type of connection that a handicapped child is unable to make.

In the meantime, what can we do for children who appear to have such handicaps? The answer is quite simple: help them make connections between what they can see and touch, and what they can say.[19]

9/ Classification and Placement

We come back finally to the issues that began this book. Are there systematic, scientifically defensible ways of detecting and treating learning disabilities? How can we tackle the overclassification problem? Is there a clear basis for deciding if a child is learning-disabled, and for evaluating his or her remedial program? Are there workable alternatives to the informal classification and placement procedures that may operate behind the scenes?

This final chapter presents my own reasoning about these questions, and my own answers to them. They are certainly not the only answers, but they are the best I have been able to formulate.

CLASSIFICATION

Funds for the special education of learning-disabled children are provided under the Education for All Handicapped Children Act. The fundamental diagnostic objective is therefore to determine whether a child is handicapped. To be in compliance with P.L. 94-142, we must be reasonably certain that an underlying, possibly incurable disorder of the central nervous system is causing the child's learning difficulties.

There is a history of resistance to the view that learning-disabled children are brain-damaged—a shift away from the views of Werner and Strauss (see Chapter 2). The term "brain-damaged" is reserved today for cases of externally caused injuries, otherwise known as acquired cerebral trauma. Even the term "minimally brain-damaged" (MBD) is no longer used with reference to learning-disabled children. Instead, the term "brain dysfunction" is preferred, in part because it carries the implication that a learning-disabled brain may be different without actually being damaged—it may have a super-developed right hemisphere, for example. But, as we saw in Chapter 5, very wide differences in brain structure and function do not in themselves produce learning handicaps. If a difference constitutes a handicap, then, according to neuropsychologists, it must have been precipitated (along with the anomalous structure) by underlying brain pathology.

Whatever terms we use—brain dysfunction, brain pathology, minimal brain damage, or neurological impairment—they all indicate that something has happened to the brain. Certain neurons or "constellations" of neurons (to use Luria's term) aren't working properly. They may be scarred, or stunted, or may biochemically malfunction, or they may even have been destroyed. The dysfunctional cells may be widely distributed or tightly localized. Impairments of this type can arise from many causes, not just from head trauma.[1] Neural injury can be caused by sudden changes in motion, such as slamming on car brakes, or from violent shaking—a major source of brain damage in cases of child abuse.[2] Injury can be caused by nutritional factors as well as by toxins such as lead.[3] It can follow illnesses, especially those with prolonged high fevers.[4] It may be associated with auto-immune defects such as diabetes, asthma, severe allergies, and rheumatoid arthritis.[5] It can occur prior to birth or during the process of birth.[6] It can be triggered by faulty genetic instructions.[7]

A first step in determining if a child has a learning handicap is therefore an examination of the child's medical history. A second step is examining the child's schoolwork and test protocols for signs of dyslexia, dysgraphia, constructional dyspraxia, and dyscalculia. (Examples of these signs are in Chapters 5, 6, 7, and 8.) The signs may be picked up by teachers and parents, and will appear on tests that are used by school diagnosticians, provided that errors are recorded. Writing and spelling errors will be recorded by the child, but the examiner will need to make phonetic records of reading errors. The three subtests on the Wide Range Achievement Test (WRAT)—Reading (word recognition), Spelling, and Arithmetic—lend themselves well to turning up these signs. So do the Letter-Word Identification, Word Attack, Calculation, Dictation, and Writing Sample subtests on the Woodcock-Johnson Tests of Achievement.

What the evaluator looks for in the reading and spelling tests are representational errors, of the sort described in Chapter 6. These indicate that the child has difficulty maintaining the aural and visual patterns of words. In contrast, rule-based errors show that a child maintains the patterns but pronounces them incorrectly, or misspells them phonetically. The child is following the wrong pronunciation or spelling rules. Representational errors are more serious. They signify that the underlying problems are more severe.[8]

I have found it useful to compare the reading errors on two word-recognition tests: the Letter-Word Identification test of the Woodcock-Johnson, and the Reading test of the WRAT. The Woodcock-Johnson test presents its words in a vertical column. They are printed in bold type and widely spaced. The WRAT reading test presents its words in horizontal rows resembling printed text, although the words do not form phrases or sentences. On the WRAT, as in regular text, words are in peripheral and focal vision simultaneously, whereas peripheral stimuli are much reduced on the Woodcock-Johnson. Eye movements (saccades) on the WRAT are more like natural reading eye movements. If a child is inclined to make representational errors, he is likely to make more of them on the WRAT Reading test, and it is often possible to identify pieces of peripheral words (or of perseverating previously read words) that are intruding into the child's focal vision.

Similarly, it can be useful to compare the child's performance on the Woodcock-Johnson Calculation test with his performance on the WRAT Arithmetic test. The Woodcock-Johnson is untimed, and provides the child with a worksheet which separates each problem into a box of its own. The WRAT Arithmetic test is timed (which is to say, the child is put under time pressure), and the test items are jumbled together on a page, as they often are on school worksheets. If a child has difficulties with the verbal/spatial requirements of arithmetic, he is likely to display more of them on the WRAT test.

The Writing Sample subtest of the Woodcock-Johnson affords a good opportunity to check for the kinds of spelling errors made when a child's attention is divided between spelling and composition (as compared to taking a spelling test). Additionally, there may be signs of grammatical difficulties—poor syntax, incorrect word endings, and so forth, as illustrated by Dave's writing in Figure 17.

Test manuals for the Woodcock-Johnson and the WRAT do not provide scoring rules or norms for the types of errors I have described. The tests are scored only for the number of correct answers, not for the characteristics of wrong answers. This is primarily because of the academic divisions that currently exist between the fields of cognitive psychology and neuropsychology on the one hand, and the field of psychometrics (test development) on the other. The people who develop and publish tests are not in close contact with the people who study how minds process test questions. This separation is rapidly diminishing, however. Standardized tests will eventually incorporate up-to-date knowledge of the cognitive processes involved in answering test questions. In the meantime, error analysis can be conducted only informally, and must be supplemented by formal quantitative diagnostic procedures.

DETERMINING SPECIFICITY

The neurological impairments that cause learning disabilities may be general or specific. That is, they may affect almost every kind of learning and thinking a child engages in, or they may affect only a specific task like spelling. In the general case, the child's IQ will be lowered. All of the tasks that the child performs on an IQ test will show deficits, as will all school tasks. If the impairment is specific, the child will perform most IQ tasks normally, and will display deficits only on particular school tasks.

The distinction between generalized and specific learning disabilities has been a source of long-standing controversy in the field. In the days of Strauss and Werner, it was taken for granted that many learning-disabled children (then called "exogenous") would have low IQs—an inevitable accompaniment of widespread brain damage. In ensuing years, however, the view arose that only children of normal intelligence who displayed severe but narrowly defined impairments should be called learning-disabled. As I pointed out in Chapter 1, this shift arose in part from budgetary policies. If children are severely enough impaired to be classified as retarded, funds for their special education are available from other budgets and need not be drawn from the learning-disabilities budget. Hence, to be eligible for funds from the learning-disabilities budget, a child must have learning problems that meet tests of specificity.

The tests differ from state to state. I am most familiar with those developed by the state of Delaware, which are similar to those used in Iowa, Kansas, Minnesota, Montana, Vermont, and Washington, among others.[9] These states use a statistical method called regression analysis that enables examiners to specify the achievement test score predicted for a given IQ. If a child's achievement test score falls below the predicted level by a specified cutoff amount, the child is said to show a severe discrepancy in that particular area, and can be classified as learning-disabled. Such specificity tests are often called severe discrepancy tests.

The cutoff score is determined statistically. It depends upon the rarity of the observed discrepancy between IQ and achievement in the population. The rarity differs for different IQ levels. Because of statistical properties of the tests, a child of high IQ is more likely than a child of low IQ to have achievement test scores below his IQ level. A child with an IQ of 125 (in the 95th percentile) will not be classified as displaying a severe discrepancy unless her achievement test scores are 30 percentile points lower. A child with an IQ of 90 (25th percentile) will be classified as showing a severe discrepancy if her achievement test scores are only 17 percentile points lower. This may strike some readers as unfair, but in fact it is much fairer than fixed-level discrepancy tests.[10]

The choice of IQ tests and achievement tests also differs from state to state, and sometimes from district to district. The IQ test most often used is the Wechsler Intelligence Test for Children–Revised (WISC-R), and the achievement test most often used is the Wide Range Achievement Test (WRAT). I am a strong advocate of more comprehensive achievement testing; at the University of Delaware we also use the Woodcock-Johnson Tests of Achievement–Revised. The Woodcock-Johnson battery includes three reading tests, two mathematics tests, two writing tests, and three tests which assess general knowledge in the domains of science, social studies, and the humanities. A comprehensive picture of a child's academic achievement is essential to sound planning.

INTERPRETING IQ TESTS

Extensive and general neurological impairment will inevitably lower IQ. The child simply cannot do the tasks on the IQ test. A child with a narrow impairment may be unable to do a specific school task (like reading) but is presumed able to do the IQ tasks normally. Is this a defensible presumption? Can an IQ test be a true measure of intelligence when a child has any sort of learning disability, no matter how narrowly defined? This question has troubled parents and professionals alike.

To begin with, the IQ tests in widespread use are not true measures of anyone's intelligence. They were not designed for that purpose, odd as that may sound; instead, they were designed for the purpose of predicting achievement in traditional academic programs. To understand this, you need to know how IQ tests are constructed. The procedures were invented by Alfred Binet in the late nineteenth century and have not changed in principle since that time.

First, the test designers assemble several thousand questions—any questions that anyone can think of.

There is no theoretical basis for the questions. In particular, questions are not drawn from contemporary cognitive or neuropsychological research programs. The current form of the WISC-R was copyrighted twenty years ago, and many of the questions on it go back forty years or more to earlier versions. (A new form of the test, known as the WISC-III, is now available, and many of the old items have been retained.) Then the initial batch of several thousand questions are administered to a sample of children for whom school grades are available. Some percentage of the questions will covary with school grades; that is, when a child's score on a test question has been high, the child's school grades will also have been high. When test scores are low, school grades will also have been low. Any test question that does not show such covariation is deleted from the test.

Such tests are good predictors of school achievement because only those items that were proven predictors were retained. No one knows what the items are really measuring. No one knows what traditional school programs really impart, either. The most we can know is that a child who is in the average range on an IQ test is likely to be in the average range in a traditional school program, a child who is below average on the IQ test is likely to do below-average schoolwork, and a child who is above average on an IQ test is likely to do above-average schoolwork.

Once we understand what IQ tests are really telling us, it is easier to decide if the information is valuable. The answer is quite often yes. It is useful to be able to tell parents: "This child has an IQ that's solidly in the average range, and he shouldn't have any trouble with regular schoolwork. If he is having problems, the source of them must be somewhere in the school or family situation. The source is not in the child's basic academic aptitude." Or, "This child ought to be in a gifted program." Or, "This child needs to be in a less competitive academic program where she won't experience so much failure."

It is important to recognize that such recommendations are as valid for learning-disabled children as they are for nondisabled children. Whatever factors operate to raise or lower a child's score on IQ test questions will also operate to raise or lower a child's performance on school tasks. The same children who took the IQ test (metaphorically speaking) are also in the child's class. The child's ranking in the IQ group and her ranking in the classroom group will remain about the same, because that's the way the IQ test was constructed. IQ information can thus be very helpful, for example, in protecting a learning-disabled child from misclassification as retarded. In fact, IQ tests in their present form originated historically with exactly that concern.

IQ TESTS AND LEARNING DISABILITIES:
A HISTORICAL NOTE

The method of IQ test construction described above was originated by Alfred Binet, a remarkable French psychologist.[11] In 1904, Binet was commissioned by the director of public education to develop ways of identifying children who needed special help in school. These included both retarded children and children who were being misclassified as retarded—children we would now classify as learning-disabled. Using the intelligence test he had developed, Binet was able to identify a child of normal intelligence who was probably afflicted with what we would now call dyslexia. He recognized the difference between specific difficulties with reading or calculating, and general academic ability:

Germaine, a child of eleven years . . . came back from a Paris school. Her parents, having [moved] to Levallois-Perret, had sent their child to one of the schools for girls in that city. But the directress refused little Germaine under the pretext that her school was full; in reality because the child was extremely backward [academically]. In fact [her academic retardation] was at least three years; her reading was hesitating, almost syllabic; faults of orthography spoiled her dictation exercise. . . . Her number work was equally poor. She was asked, "If I have 19 apples, and eat 6 of them, how many have I left?" The child, reckoning mentally, said "12" which is inexact but reasonable. Trying it on paper, she was lost; she made an addition instead of subtraction and found 25. In other calculations she showed that she had the power to reckon mentally, but not on paper. . . . On the other hand her wide awake and mischievous air, and the vivacity of her speech made a favorable impression upon us. We made the test of intelligence and showed that her intelligence was normal; she was backward [on the intelligence test] scarcely a year. This is a characteristic example which shows the use of our measuring scale.[12]

Some of the items on Binet's original scale are still found on IQ scales of today. Since traditional school programs haven't changed much, it hasn't been necessary to change traditional IQ tests either.[13]

PLACEMENT

To show how all this information is put together in making placement recommendations, I'll present two cases from my own practice.

KATHY

Kathy was eight years old when tested. Her medical history included treatment for strabismus (an eye-muscle problem) during kindergarten, and recent diagnosis of a rare autoimmunological disorder which also afflicted her father. Her family history included references to cousins on her mother's side who were diagnosed as dyslexic, and her father's statement that he learned to read only by memorizing the shapes of words. (Father has a Ph.D. in chemistry.) Kathy is talented in art and athletics. She was referred for testing because of difficulties in learning to read and spell.

Kathy's test scores are shown in Table 11. They are presented as percentiles, standard scores, and grade levels—three ways of transforming raw scores to show how they compare to scores of other children the same age.[14] Kathy's Full Scale IQ is 132, which is in the Very Superior category. The Full Scale IQ can be subdivided into a Verbal IQ and a Performance IQ, which in Kathy's case are quite far apart. This difference in scores is rare in the population (as are artistic talents), but it does not indicate underlying brain pathology, nor does it predict specific achievement discrepancies.

Kathy's discrepancy pattern is revealed by comparing her Full Scale IQ to her achievement test scores. The standard scores for reading, writing, and spelling are much lower than the scores on mathematics and general knowledge. Asterisks indicate scores that meet the State of Delaware's severe discrepancy criteria. Under the time pressure of the WRAT, Kathy's arithmetic score also dropped below the discrepancy cutoff, although her standard score on the untimed Woodcock-Johnson calculation test was well above the cutoff. Notably, Kathy made errors on the WRAT arithmetic test that she did not make on the Woodcock-Johnson. For example, working under the WRAT time pressures and spatially crowded conditions, Kathy lost her sense of direction on subtraction problems.

Table 11. Kathy's Test Scores

Test	Standard score	Percentile	Grade level
WISC-R			
Verbal IQ	111	77	—
Performance IQ	147	99	—
Full Scale IQ	132	98	—
Woodcock-Johnson			
Reading			
Letter-Word	89*	24	2.6
Word Attack	75*	5	1.3
Passage Comprehension	95*	37	2.8
Written Language			
Dictation	82*	12	1.8
Writing Samples	74*	4	1.6
Mathematics			
Calculation (untimed)	114	82	4.3
Applied Problems	120	91	5.4
General Knowledge			
Science	109	72	4.5
Social Studies	116	87	5.4
Humanities	105	64	4.2
Wide Range Achievement Test			
Reading	73*	4	2B
Spelling	79*	8	2M
Arithmetic	94*	34	2E

B=beginning level of grade; M=middle; E=end. *Severe discrepancy by Delaware's criteria.

Here are our recommendations to her parents:

Kathy should be placed in a remedial program that has been designed for dyslexics—one that explicitly teaches letter-sound correspondence rules, and that provides extensive practice in applying them. It is important to understand that conventional methods of reading instruction do not work with dyslexics. The dyslexic child needs special training in dealing with the connections between letters and sounds, just as a blind child needs to learn braille, and a deaf child needs to learn sign language.

It is extremely important not to place this bright child in any class for slow learners, not even in reading. She should be maintained in a challenging educational environment, commensurate with her mental abilities. This means also that she should never be removed from classwork in the content areas (science, for example) for remedial reading.

As Kathy grows older, more and more academic information will have to be acquired through reading. Her age group is just now beginning to "read to learn" as compared with "learning to read." It is imperative to find ways of providing Kathy with information that she cannot obtain for herself through reading. For example, her reading assignments can be read aloud to her and discussed with her. Activities that extend her information in non-reading ways (visiting museums, watching educational TV, etc.) should be regularly planned.

At the same time, Kathy should be encouraged to keep trying to learn from books. There are a number of ways in which both school and home can provide "scaffolding" for Kathy without reducing intellectual challenge. Her reading assignments can sometimes be read aloud *with* her, rather than *to* her. This enables her to participate in the complete reading process. Otherwise, her attention to meaning (an important part of the reading process) will be deflected by her attempts to decode words for herself. This same procedure should be followed when stories, comics, etc., are read. Additionally, the ideas behind the reading material should be discussed with her. She should be encouraged to make inferences about meaning and about words. At the same time, she should see the print, and follow a moving finger as the words are read aloud. The amount of this supported reading should be as extensive as possible. As long as her interest can be maintained, it is impossible to do too much of this. The level of difficulty of the material should not be a consideration. Read to Kathy from adult encyclopedias if those are what interest her. Supported reading is important not only because it will help strengthen skills, but also because it will keep Kathy mindful of the joys of reading, so that she will understand the value of making the effort to become a good reader.

In talking to Kathy about her difficulties, parents and teachers should make sure she understands that she is not "dumb," and that her reading problems are not her fault. She needs to understand that reading problems sometimes run in families, and other people in her family had difficulties learning to read, too. If she comes "to college" [the University of Delaware's remedial reading program] over the year, she will meet other children who have the same kinds of problems, and they will all work together to learn new ways of reading and writing that have helped hundreds of other children, and will help Kathy as well.

Finally, it is going to be important throughout Kathy's schooling to provide her with training in the visual arts and related skills. Kathy's gift needs as much educational attention as her handicap does. Additionally, her pattern-recognition skills are crucial compensatory avenues of learning. Geometry, for example, can be taught visually or taught verbally, as a list of rules. It is clearly of the utmost importance to teach Kathy visually, to the greatest extent possible. Even in reading, for example, encourage her to visualize characters and events. In social studies, let her draw maps and diagrams and pictures, and help her to find ways of visually representing abstractions like "democracy."

NEILL

Neill was 16 years old when tested. His medical history included vision problems which had been unrecognized and uncorrected during the later elementary years.

His family history revealed that his sister had reading problems, and that his father does not read. Neill is talented in sports, but at the time of testing he was banned from the playing fields because he had failed English and biology. Throughout his school history Neill had been considered a "slow learner" but had never been classified as learning-disabled. He was finally referred for testing at the insistence of a high school remedial reading teacher who felt that Neill's reading, spelling, and handwriting problems were out of the ordinary.

Table 12 shows that Neill's Full Scale IQ is 84, which is in the Low Average category. He is severely discrepant, by Delaware's criteria, on most reading and spelling tests, and he displayed representational and syntactic errors that his teacher had correctly recognized as exceptional. Notably, however, Neill's Passage Comprehension score is commensurate with his IQ. This is the same phenomenon we saw in Dave's case (see Chapter 6). Children who cannot reliably decode individual words may nevertheless, over the years, construct strategies for figuring out what a passage means—or at least for figuring out how to answer questions on comprehension tests.[15]

Here are our recommendations to Neill's parents:

First and foremost, Neill's school should put him back on the playing fields. His reading and writing problems are not his fault, and he cannot fix them, any more than a blind person can fix his sight, or a deaf person can fix his hearing. The kinds of remedial help that Neill needs (to be explained below) do not require time off from sports. On the contrary, sports are Neill's primary avenue to success, and the opportunity to participate in them is an essential motivating factor. Sports will keep Neill in school so that the school can, at long last, provide him with the special education he needs.

Neill should be strongly commended for the courage he

Table 12. Neill's Test Scores

Test	Standard score	Percentile	Grade level
WISC-R			
Verbal IQ	84	14	—
Performance IQ	87	19	—
Full Scale IQ	84	14	—
Woodcock-Johnson			
Reading			
Letter-Word	68*	2	3.3
Word Attack	41*	below 1	1.1
Passage Comprehension	81	10	5.1
Written Language			
Dictation	66*	1	3.7
Writing Samples	39*	below 1	1.5
Mathematics			
Calculation (untimed)	89	24	7.3
Applied Problems	85	15	5.8
General Knowledge			
Science	78	7	3.8
Social Studies	80	9	5.8
Humanities	76	6	3.2
Wide Range Achievement Test			
Reading	62*	1	3B
Spelling	66*	1	3E
Arithmetic (timed)	74	4	6E

B=beginning level of grade; E=end. *Severe discrepancy by Delaware's criteria.

has displayed in trying to meet school requirements, despite a handicap that no one, including Neill himself, knew he had. Neill should be assured that he is not stupid (he has probably been worried about that), and that his reading problems are not his fault. From now on, he should find that dealing with school will be less stressful. People will be helping him develop strategies for learning and remembering written material, and will be making accommodations for his special difficulties with reading and writing.

Neill should immediately be assigned a "reading and writing partner" (perhaps one from each class) who can read all his assignments aloud to him, and with him. To the extent that it is possible, Neill should read out loud with his partner, so that he is hearing the right words and the right intonation patterns and seeing the words at the same time. This kind of assisted reading will prevent Neill from missing meaning due to the distraction of trying, by himself, to decode words. Let him decode as best he can, while hearing how the text should sound. After the materials have been read, Neill's partner can help him write out assignments. Neill should first dictate what he wants to say, and should then edit and clarify what his partner has written down. Alternatively, if this is possible, Neill should write with his partner. They can then compare notes and produce a final version.

Neill should be similarly assisted to read and write arithmetic. He should listen to and then repeat problems, dictate what he thinks the answer should be, and then practice writing it out.

Neill should be permitted to take examinations orally, or to have unlimited time, and a reader-proctor, for written examinations.

Regarding his reading and spelling instruction, Neill should be provided immediately, at the school's expense, with a tutor in a remedial reading program that has been designed for dyslexics—one that explicitly teaches letter-sound correspondence rules, and provides extensive practice in applying them in both reading and spelling.

Neill should be given specific instruction in handwriting, and should practice handwriting (in workbooks) for a set period of time every day.

Neill must make a special effort to acquire more information about history, politics, world affairs, literature, and the arts. This will help bring up his grades in social studies and the humanities, and it will also help him compensate for his reading handicap. A good fund of background information will help Neill figure out what a passage means, even though he doesn't recognize all of the words in it. Neill should spend some time each week watching educational television and discussing it with his parents. Family conversation should explore current events and provide practice in remembering specific names and places.

Review of earlier materials in arithmetic, science, and social studies may also be helpful. The review should begin with materials that Neill already knows and finds easy, and work up from there. The emphasis should be upon strategies, techniques for figuring out how an assignment should be done, what has to be noticed, remembered, etc. If the tutor first thinks, "Now, how would I do that?" and then teaches Neill those strategies, the tutor will be helping Neill build a mental tool kit that he can broadly apply.

CONCLUSIONS

First of all, it is essential for dyslexic children to be provided with a remedial reading program designed for dyslexics. These are programs that teach specific, strict rules for reading and spelling—rules that normal children may pick up for themselves, but that dyslexic children cannot. If such a program is not available in the school, then a trained tutor of dyslexics should be found for the child, and the cost of the tutor should be financed under P.L. 94-142. Parents must insist upon this, even though a school may want to assign the child to an ordinary remedial reading class. Such classes typically provide only alternative versions of the type of instruction that didn't work for the dyslexic child in the first place.

A second point is that these recommendations are intended not to be exhaustive, but only to illustrate the kinds of individualized help that learning-disabled youngsters really need—assistance, tutoring, and coaching on their regular classwork. All too often, they don't receive it. Instead, these children are removed from their classrooms, which means they miss lessons that are being conducted there, and are given different work in a resource room. The exact connections between the resource room lessons and regular classroom lessons are at best vague. It would be far more efficient for the resource room teacher to tutor the child directly in the work that his regular classroom teacher has assigned.

A third point is that these recommendations are useful for all children. A child doesn't have to be declared "learning-disabled" to benefit from supported reading, museums, study buddies, reviewing materials from earlier years (especially arithmetic), and the like. In fact, if parents and teachers can make such arrangements, there is probably little point even in having a child tested for learning disabilities. A home-designed or teacher-designed personalized assistance program may be far better than the standardized program that the school provides for its so-called learning-disabled pupils—many of whom were probably misclassified.

FUTURE DIRECTIONS

The classification and placement procedures that I have described illustrate the best ways we have at present of complying with P.L. 94-142. They constitute a stable platform for making workable decisions within the framework of a massive educational bureaucracy that is, like all bureaucracies, very set in its ways. The procedures I have outlined may require a few adjustments, but they are bureaucratically manageable adjustments. It is a straightforward matter to include more achievement tests (most schools don't include enough), to score test protocols for errors, to include a brief medical questionnaire (which the school nurse could administer), and to adopt a regression formula rather than a fixed-discrepancy formula for classifying children.

Eventually the science of learning disabilities will progress to the point where it can contribute new techniques for diagnosis and remediation. These will not be the simple paper-and-pencil methods used today, but high-technology brain-scanning techniques for tracking the flow of information through a child's mind. When that time comes, many of the controversies that have plagued the field will finally be resolved.

By that time as well, the school system will have changed into one that is more tolerant of differences among children. The traditional American educational system, in force for more than two hundred years now, is finally beginning to give way. We are beginning at last to see it for the antique it is, and to design schools that reflect contemporary knowledge, goals, and values.

In the meantime, when a child is not fitting into the traditional educational system, concerned parents and teachers should be wary of concluding that the child may be "learning-disabled," and of setting in motion classification machinery that has been designed solely to assess how far the child misses the traditional mark. It is better to ask first: What kind of a learning environment would this child thrive in? And, second, How can I help to provide it?

But that is another book.[16]

Notes
Credits
Index

Notes

1. This discussion has been derived from a number of sources. To begin with, there have been several studies of child study teams which address the issues of communication and team member participation. These include J. E. Gilliam and M. C. Coleman, "Who Influences IEP Committee Decisions?" *Exceptional Children* 47 (1981): 642–644; H. M. Knoff, "Investigating Disproportionate Influence and Status in Multidisciplinary Child Study Teams," *Exceptional Children* 49 (1983): 367–370; H. Mehan, J. Meihls, A. Hertwick, and M. Crowdes, "Identifying Handicapped Students," in *Organizational Behavior in Schools and School Districts*, ed. S. B. Bacharach (New York: Praeger, 1981); and a recent dissertation conducted under my supervision, which compared communication processes in IEP meetings in a mid-Atlantic setting to those in rural Alaska, serving Inupiat Eskimo: M. P. Lucas, *Child Study Team Meetings: Appropriateness in Cross-Cultural Settings*, University of Delaware, 1991. These studies all indicate that decisions about the children are made primarily by school personnel prior to the meeting with the parents, and that the IEP is written in advance, which is in direct violation of the law—see, for example, *Spielberg v. Henrico County Public Schools*, 853 F.2d 256 (4th Cir. 1988). Much of the documentation of informal classification processes has

been conducted by James Ysseldyke and his colleagues. A summary paper that includes a number of additional references is Bob Algozzine and James Ysseldyke, "The Future of the LD Field: Screening and Diagnosis," *Journal of Learning Disabilities* 19 (1986): 394–398. See also Susan Epps, James Ysseldyke, and Matt McGue, "'I Know One When I See One': Differentiating LD and non-LD Students," *Learning Disability Quarterly* 7 (1984): 89–101; and Martha Thurlow, James Ysseldyke, and Ann Casey, "Teachers' Perceptions of Criteria for Identifying Learning Disabled Students," *Psychology in the Schools* 21 (1984): 349–355. Regarding the match between the IEP and the child's actual needs, see my "Time Now for a Little Serious Complexity," in *Handbook of Cognitive, Social, and Neuropsychological Aspects of Learning Disabilities,* ed. S. J. Ceci (Hillsdale, N.J.: Erlbaum, 1986). For recent documentation concerning the extent to which the IEPs are actually implemented, see S. W. Smith, "Comparison of Individualized Education Programs (IEPs) of Students with Behavioral Disorder and Learning Disabilities," *Journal of Special Education* 24 (1990): 85–100. Smith reports that "in a large number of cases IEP teams did not provide unique and individualized instructional programs for students . . . A substantial number of IEPs written for students with learning disabilities and behavioral disorders failed to function as effective instructional guides" (p. 97).

2. *Learning Disabilities: A Report to the United States Congress* (1987). This report was submitted by the Interagency Committee on Learning Disabilities, chaired by James Wyngaarden, Director of the National Institutes of Health. The committee represented thirteen government agencies: National Institute of Child Health and Human Development, National Institute of Neurological and Communicative Disorders and Stroke, National Institute of Allergy and Infectional Diseases, National Eye Institute, National Institute of Environmental Health Sciences, Division of Research Resources, Food and Drug Administration, Na-

tional Institute of Mental Health, Centers for Disease Control, Environmental Protection Agency, Health Resources and Services Administration, Office of Human Development Services, and Department of Education. Each of these agencies does work that bears on learning disabilities and needs to estimate the extent and cost of the problem as each agency deals with it. The report contains the most authoritative estimates of prevalence that I have been able to find.

3. As we will see, the classification of a child as learning-disabled implies that he or she suffers from a central nervous system dysfunction which is for practical purposes incurable. While there has been a reluctance to use terms like "brain damage" to characterize a learning-disabled child, the fact is that something happened, before birth or afterward, that impaired the child's brain. Of course, nothing may have impaired the brains of children who are *mis*classified as learning-disabled. That is exactly my point. Misclassifications, no matter how well intentioned, carry very serious medical implications.

4. W. Alan Davis and Lorrie Shepard, "Specialists' Use of Tests and Clinical Judgment in the Diagnosis of Learning Disabilities," *Learning Disability Quarterly* 6 (1983): 128–138. The abstract reads: "Five hundred and forty-two learning-disabilities teachers, 130 school psychologists, and 179 speech/language teachers in Colorado were surveyed. Although [the specialists] generally preferred tests with higher reliability and validity, poor tests were still used frequently even when superior substitutes were available. All groups of specialists tended to overrate the tests they used and generally indicated a lack of familiarity with the psychometric properties of commonly used tests. Although a majority of specialists valued clinical judgment over test scores (see Epps et al., "I Know One When I See One"), substantial numbers appeared to lack knowledge of procedures to ensure the validity of such judgments. One-third to one-half of each specialist group could

not correctly interpret ability-achievement score discrepancies" upon which LD classifications are often based.

5. Untimed SAT scores predict higher college grades than the students achieve. College grades are better predicted by timed SAT scores. This is especially true in the case of learning-disabled students. H. Braun, M. Ragosta, and B. Kaplan, "The Predictive Validity of the Scholastic Aptitude Test for Disabled Students," Research Report RR-86-38, Educational Testing Service, Princeton, N.J.

6. Reviews of these issues may be found in the following papers: James Chalfant, "Learning Disabilities: Policy Issues and Promising Approaches," *American Psychologist* (February 1989): 392–398; James Gallagher, "Learning Disabilities and Special Education: A Critique," *Journal of Learning Disabilities* 19 (1986): 595–601; Michael Gerber and Melvyn Semmel, "Teacher as Imperfect Test: Reconceptualizing the Referral Process," *Educational Psychologist* 19 (1984): 137–148; and Joseph Torgesen, "Learning Disabilities Theory: Its Current State and Future Prospects," *Journal of Learning Disabilities* 19 (1986): 399–407.

7. United States Office of Education, "Procedures for Evaluating Specific Learning Disabilities," *Federal Register* 42 (1977): 65082–65085.

8. National Joint Committee on Learning Disabilities, "Learning Disabilities: Issues on Definition," 1981; reprinted in *Journal of Learning Disabilities* 20 (1987): 107–108. This was updated by the National Joint Committee on Learning Disabilities in "Topic: Modifications to the NJCLD Definition of Learning Disabilities," *Letter from NJCLD to Member Organizations,* September 18, 1989. The National Joint Committee is composed of the following organizations: American Speech-Language-Hearing Association, Learning Disability Association of America (formerly the National Association for Children and Adults with Learning Disabilities), Council for Learning Disabilities, Division for Learning Disabilities, International Reading Association, National Association of School Psychologists, and Orton Dyslexia Society. The issue of definition

has caused raging disagreement. For an exceptionally clear and rational summary of the current situation, see Donald Hammill, "On Defining Learning Disabilities: An Emerging Consensus," *Journal of Learning Disabilities* 23 (1990), 74–84.

9. The data in this section are taken from Michael Gerber, "Is Congress Getting the Full Story?" *Exceptional Children* 51 (1984): 209–224; "Educating All Children: Ten Years Later," *Exceptional Children* 56 (1989): 17–27; and Judith Singer and John Butler, "The Education for All Handicapped Children Act: Schools as Agents of Social Reform," *Harvard Educational Review* 57 (1987): 125–152.

10. *A Nation at Risk* (Washington, D.C.: U.S. Government Printing Office, 1983) came to the alarming conclusion that "the educational foundations of our society are presently being eroded by a rising tide of mediocrity that threatens our very future as a nation and as a people . . . If an unfriendly foreign power had attempted to impose on America the mediocre educational performance that exists today, we might well have viewed it as an act of war." SAT scores fell 68 points from 1967 to 1981, gained back 16 points by 1985, leveled off, and then began dropping again in 1988 (*National Report on College Bound Seniors*, published yearly by the Educational Testing Service, Princeton, N.J.).

11. *The Reading Report Card, 1971–1988*, Report No. 19-R-01, Educational Testing Service, Princeton, N.J.

12. Edward Fiske, "American Students Score Average or Below in International Math Exams," *New York Times*, September 23, 1984; K. C. Cole, "Science Under Scrutiny," *New York Times, Education Life*, January 7, 1990.

13. This is clearly my bias, and I have documented it extensively in another book in this series, *Schooling* (Cambridge, Mass.: Harvard University Press, 1990). This book details a new apprenticeship approach to education. If classrooms were designed along the lines that I propose in that book, then children of all kinds, including children with severe handicaps, could be productively integrated into them.

14. Benjamin Bloom, "The 2-Sigma Problem: The Search for

Methods of Group Instruction as Effective as One-to-One Tutoring," *Educational Researcher* 13 (1984): 4–16.

2 / ORIGINS OF THE FIELD

1. Kurt Goldstein, *Aftereffects of Brain Injuries in War* (New York: Grune & Stratton, 1942).
2. Alfred Strauss and Laura S. Lehtinen, *Psychopathology and Education of the Brain-Injured Child* (New York: Grune & Stratton, 1947).
3. Karl S. Lashley, *Brain Mechanisms and Intelligence* (New York: Dover, 1963).
4. J. J. McCarthy and Joan F. McCarthy, *Learning Disabilities* (Boston: Allyn and Bacon, 1963). The quotation, in a letter from Lehtinen, appears on p. 29.
5. H. G. Birch, ed., *Brain Damage in Children: The Biological and Social Aspects* (Baltimore: Williams & Wilkins, 1964), p. 6. Herbert Birch was first of all a very good experimental psychologist, a Ph.D. in physiological psychology. Later, he got a medical degree, specializing in pediatric neurology.
6. Heinz Werner, *Comparative Psychology of Mental Development* (1948; rept., New York: Science Editions, 1961).
7. All the quotations in this paragraph are from Werner, *Comparative Psychology of Mental Development*, p. 297.
8. Doris Carrison and Heinz Werner, "Principles and Methods of Teaching Arithmetic to Mentally Retarded Children," *American Journal of Mental Deficiency* 47 (1943): 309–317.
9. Heinz Werner, "Development of Visuo-Motor Performance on the Marble-Board Test in Mentally Retarded Children," *Journal of Genetic Psychology* 64 (1944): 269–279.
10. Alfred Strauss and Heinz Werner, "Disorders of Conceptual Thinking in the Brain-Injured Child," *Journal of Nervous and Mental Disease* 96 (1942): 153–172.
11. W. M. Cruickshank, *The Brain-Injured Child in Home, School and Community* (Syracuse: Syracuse University Press, 1967).

12. M. Critchley, *The Dyslexic Child* (London: Heinemann, 1970).

13. James Hinshelwood, *Congenital Word-Blindness* (London: Lewis, 1917).

14. James Hinshelwood, "A Case of Dyslexia: A Peculiar Form of Word-Blindness," *Lancet* 2 (1896): 1451–1454.

15. Ibid., p. 1453.

16. James Hinshelwood, "A Case of 'Word' Without 'Letter' Blindness," *Lancet* 1 (1898): 422–425.

17. James Kerr, "School Hygiene, in its Mental, Moral and Physical Aspects," Howard Medal Prize Essay, *Journal of the Royal Statistical Society* 60 (1897): 613–680.

18. James Hinshelwood, "Word-Blindness and Visual Memory," *Lancet* (1895): 1564–1570.

19. W. Pringle Morgan, "A Case of Congenital Word-Blindness," *British Medical Journal* 2 (1896): 1378.

20. James Hinshelwood, "The Visual Memory for Words and Figures," *British Medical Journal* 2 (1896): 1543–1544.

21. Hinshelwood, *Congenital Word-Blindness*, pp. 49–51. There is an interesting anomaly about this case, and several others that Hinshelwood reported: some of his dyslexic readers were alleged to be good writers and spellers. We seldom see this today. Most dyslexics also suffer from the spelling and writing disorder known as dysgraphia. One can think of several reasons for the anomaly. First, spelling was taught differently and measured differently in the late 1800s. Second, children who could neither read nor write might have been classified as "all-round poor." Third, Hinshelwood was developing quite a complex theory of different kinds of dyslexia, each of which had its special brain location, and some of which also involved spelling and writing disorders. This particular case was only one type. Interestingly, Hinshelwood's theory that there were many different types of dyslexia and dysgraphia is receiving new support from contemporary neuropsychologists. See, for example, the descriptions of dyslexia and dysgraphia in Andrew Ellis and Andrew Young, *Human Cognitive Neuropsychology* (London: Erlbaum, 1988). A well-

known case of pure dyslexia without dysgraphia was reported in 1966 by Norman Geschwind, "Color-Naming Defects in Association with Alexia," *Archives of Neurology* 15 (1966): 137–146.

22. Samuel T. Orton, "'Word-Blindness' in School Children," *Archives of Neurology and Psychiatry* 14 (1925): 582–615.

23. Samuel T. Orton, *Reading, Writing, and Speech Problems in Children* (New York: Norton, 1937).

24. Orton, "Word-Blindness," pp. 607, 608.

25. As the field has evolved, only syndromes 1 and 2 are still considered learning disabilities. Syndromes 3 and 4 are classified as speech disorders, and syndrome 5 as a motor disorder, probably mild cerebral palsy. For this reason I do not discuss syndromes 3, 4, and 5 in this book.

26. J. Lee Wiederholt, "Historical Perspectives in the Education of the Learning Disabled," in L. Mann and D. Sabatino, eds., *The Second Review of Special Education* (Philadelphia: Journal of Special Education Press, 1974).

3 / THE TRANSITIONAL PERIOD

1. Samuel A. Kirk, "Behavioral Diagnosis and Remediation of Learning Disabilities," in *Proceedings of the Annual Meeting of the Conference on Exploration into the Problems of the Perceptually Handicapped Child,* vol. 1 (Chicago, 1963).

2. Ibid.

3. Daniel P. Hallahan and William M. Cruickshank, *Psychoeducational Foundations of Learning Disabilities* (Englewood Cliffs, N.J.: Prentice-Hall, 1973). Chap. 1 contains portions of the text of Kirk's 1963 speech, and explains the reactions of some of his professional colleagues and of parent groups.

4. Samuel A. Kirk and Winifred D. Kirk, *Psycholinguistic Learning Disabilities: Diagnosis and Remediation* (Urbana: University of Illinois Press, 1971).

5. Anne Anastasi, *Differential Psychology* (New York: Macmillan, 1967).

6. A. Jean Ayres, *Sensory Integration and Learning Disorders* (Los Angeles: Western Psychological Services, 1972). The

tests described in this section may be obtained from Western Psychological Services. See also A. Jean Ayres, "Improving Academic Scores through Sensory Integration," *Journal of Learning Disabilities* 5 (1972): 338–342, and "The Sensorimotor Foundations of Academic Ability," in *Perceptual and Learning Disabilities in Children*, vol. 2, ed. W. M. Cruickshank and D. P. Hallahan (New York: Syracuse University Press, 1975).

7. Newell C. Kephart, *The Slow Learner in the Classroom* (Columbus: Merrill, 1971), was Kephart's most famous book. His work at the Wayne County Training School is also published in Alfred A. Strauss and Newell C. Kephart, *Psychopathology and Education of the Brain-Injured Child* (New York: Grune & Stratton, 1955).

8. The perceptual-motor match is an example of a servomechanism. For a highly readable account of how the concept of servomechanisms was beginning to enter into psychological theorizing during the period when Kephart was formulating his own views, see George A. Miller, Eugene Galanter, and Karl H. Pribram, *Plans and the Structure of Behavior* (New York: Holt, Rinehart & Winston, 1960).

9. Marianne Frostig and P. Maslow, *Learning Problems in the Classroom* (New York: Grune & Stratton, 1973); Frostig et al., *The Marianne Frostig Developmental Test of Visual Perception*, 1963 standardization (Palo Alto, Calif.: Consulting Psychologists' Press). Figures 6 and 7 are taken from Marianne Frostig, "Visual Perception, Integrative Functions, and Academic Learning," *Journal of Learning Disabilities* 5 (1972): 5–15.

10. Samuel A. Kirk and J. Chalfant, *Academic and Developmental Learning Disabilities* (Denver: Love, 1984), provides an update on Kirk's views.

11. Regarding the Ayres program: J. F. Densem et al., "Effectiveness of a Sensory Integrative Therapy Program for Children with Perceptual-Motor Deficits," *Journal of Learning Disabilities* 22 (1989): 221–229, summarizes fourteen evaluation studies of Ayres' training approach, and concludes that the majority of the studies, including one of

their own, show that the program was not effective. Regarding Kephart and Frostig: see Donald Hammill, Libby Goodman, and J. Lee Wiederholt, "Visual-Motor Processes: Can We Train Them?" *The Reading Teacher* (February 1974): 469–478. Regarding Kirk: see D. D. Hammill and S. C. Larsen, "The Efficacy of Psycholinguistic Training," *Exceptional Children* 41 (1974): 5–14, and V. Sowell et al., "Effects of Psycholinguistic Training on Improving Psycholinguistic Skills," *Learning Disability Quarterly* 2 (1979): 69–77.

12. Carl H. Delacato, *Neurological Organization and Reading* (Springfield, Mass.: Thomas, 1966). A useful summary and critique are in P. I. Myers and D. D. Hammill, *Learning Disabilities: Basic Concepts, Assessment Practices, and Instructional Strategies* (Austin, Tex.: Pro-Ed, 1990).

13. American Academy of Pediatrics, "The Doman-Delacato Treatment of Neurologically Handicapped Children," *Pediatrics* 70 (1982): 810–812. For a detailed explanation of what is wrong with both theory and therapy, see Natalia Chapanis, "The Patterning Method of Therapy: A Critique," in Perry Black, ed., *Brain Dysfunction in Children* (New York: Raven Press, 1981).

14. Harold N. Levinson, *A Solution to the Riddle of Dyslexia* (New York: Springer-Verlag, 1980), and *Smart but Feeling Dumb* (New York: Warner, 1984).

15. J. Marshall, "Review of *Dyslexia: A Solution to the Riddle*," *Journal of Research in Reading* 6 (1983): 62–73. According to Marshall, Levinson's book is "the most brilliant parody of clinical research this reviewer has ever read . . . The movie version, directed by Mel Brooks and starring Zero Mostel, should be spectacular" (pp. 72–73). For a review of other research on possible vestibular dysfunction in learning-disabled children, see H. J. Polatajko, "A Critical Look at Vestibular Dysfunction in Learning-Disabled Children," *Developmental Medicine and Child Neurology* 27 (1985): 283–292.

16. P. V. Carlson and N. K. Greenspoon, "The Uses and Abuses of Visual Training for Children with Perceptual-Motor Learning Problems," *American Journal of Optometry* 45

(1968): 161–169. For a comprehensive review of optometric vision training programs, see B. K. Keogh and M. Pelland, "Vision Training Revisited," *Journal of Learning Disabilities* 18 (1985): 228–236.

17. R. L. Metzger and D. B. Werner, "Use of Visual Training for Reading Disabilities: A Review," *Pediatrics* 73 (1984): 824–829. Eye movements are a major focus of study by experimental psychologists and vision researchers. For an authoritative review of basic research on the role of eye movements in reading and dyslexia, see Marcel Just and Patricia Carpenter, *The Psychology of Reading and Language Comprehension* (Boston: Allyn and Bacon, 1987).

18. American Academy of Pediatrics, "Joint Positional Statement: The Eye and Learning Disabilities," *Pediatrics* 49 (1972): 454–455.

19. C. A. Ferreri and R. B. Wainwright, *Breakthrough for Dyslexia and Learning Disabilities* (Pompano Beach: Exposition Press of Florida, 1984).

20. Larry B. Silver, "The 'Magic Cure': A Review of the Current Controversial Approaches for Treating Learning Disabilities," *Journal of Learning Disabilities* 20 (1987): 498–504.

21. For another perspective on the history of the field, and especially for information about its political struggles, see Joseph Torgesen, "Learning Disabilities: Historical and Conceptual Issues," in *Learning About Learning Disabilities*, ed. B. Y. L. Wong (San Diego: Academic Press, 1991).

4 / INFORMATION PROCESSING RESEARCH

1. William James, *Talks to Teachers* (1899; rept., New York: Norton, 1958), p. 28.

2. Bernard Baars, *The Cognitive Revolution in Psychology* (New York: Guilford Press, 1986); George A. Miller, "What Is Information Measurement?" *American Psychologist* 8 (1953): 3–11.

3. George Sperling, "The Information Available in Brief Visual Perceptions," *Psychological Monographs* 74 (1960), no. 11.

4. Saul Sternberg, "Memory-Scanning: Mental Processes Revealed by Reaction Time Experiments," *American Scientist* 57 (1969): 421–457.
5. William Chase, "Elementary Information Processes," in *Handbook of Learning and Cognitive Processes*, vol. 5, ed. W. K. Estes (Hillsdale, N.J.: Erlbaum, 1978).
6. S. Kosslyn, *Ghosts in the Mind's Machine* (New York: Norton, 1983).
7. Earl Hunt, "Mechanics of Verbal Ability," *Psychological Review* 85 (1978): 109–130.
8. S. Sternberg et al., "The Latency and Duration of Rapid Movement Sequences: Comparisons of Speech and Typewriting," in *Information Processing in Motor Control and Learning*, ed. G. E. Stelmach (New York: Academic Press, 1978).
9. M. T. H. Chi, "Short-Term Memory Limitation in Children: Capacity or Processing Deficits?" *Memory & Cognition* 4 (1976): 559–572; M. T. H. Chi, "Speed of Processing: A Developmental Source of Limitation," *Topics in Learning and Learning Disabilities* 2 (1982): 23–32; M. E. Ford and D. P. Keating, "Developmental and Individual Differences in Long-Term Memory Retrieval: Process and Organization," *Child Development* 52 (1981): 234–241; Robert Kail, "Developmental Functions for Speeds of Cognitive Processes," *Journal of Experimental Child Psychology* 45 (1988): 339–364.
10. A. D. Baddeley, *Working Memory* (New York: Oxford University Press, 1986).
11. Chi, "Short-Term Memory Limitation in Children."
12. The self-programming characteristics of working memory are rigorously depicted in production-system models of human performance. It's simply not possible to go into the technicalities of this work here. Interested readers may wish to begin with Earl Hunt and S. Poltrack, "The Mechanics of Thought," in *Human Information Processing: Tutorials in Performance and Cognition*, ed. B. H. Kantowitz (Hillsdale, N.J.: Erlbaum, 1974). More recent innovations with applications to education are described in John Anderson, *The Architecture of Cognition* (Cambridge: Harvard University Press, 1983). Innovations with applications to

development, along with a helpful theoretical overview, are in David Klahr, Pat Langley, and Robert Neches, eds., *Production System Models of Learning and Development* (Cambridge: MIT Press, 1987).

13. The seminal textbook presentation of network concepts of long-term memory is Peter Lindsay and Donald Norman, *Human Information Processing* (New York: Academic Press, 1977), highly readable and still one of the best. More recent reviews may be found in any textbook of cognitive psychology, for example, Robert Solso, *Cognitive Psychology* (Boston: Allyn and Bacon, 1988). I specially recommend John Anderson, *Cognitive Psychology and Its Implications* (New York: Freeman, 1990).

14. H. Lee Swanson, "Process Assessment of Intelligence in Learning Disabled and Mentally Retarded Children: A Multidirectional Model," *Educational Psychologist* 19 (1984): 149–162; "Effects of Cognitive Effort and Word Distinctiveness on Learning Disabled and Nondisabled Readers' Recall," *Journal of Educational Psychology* 76 (1984): 894–908; "Semantic and Visual Memory Codes in Learning Disabled Readers," *Journal of Experimental Child Psychology* 37 (1984): 124–140; "Do Semantic Memory Deficiencies Underlie Learning Disabled Readers' Encoding Process?" *Journal of Experimental Child Psychology* 41 (1986): 461–488; "The Combining of Multiple Hemispheric Resources in Learning Disabled and Skilled Readers' Recall of Words: A Test of Three Information Processing Models," *Brain and Cognition* 6 (1987): 41–54.

15. H. Lee Swanson, "The Effects of Central Processing Strategies on Learning Disabled, Mildly Retarded, Average, and Gifted Children's Elaborative Encoding Abilities," *Journal of Experimental Child Psychology* 47 (1989): 370–397.

16. Richard Shiffrin and Susan Dumais, "The Development of Automatism" in *Cognitive Skills and Their Acquisition*, ed. John Anderson (Hillsdale, N.J.: Erlbaum, 1981).

17. Richard H. Bauer and J. Emhert, "Information Processing in Reading-Disabled and Nondisabled Children," *Journal of Experimental Child Psychology* 37 (1984): 271–281.

18. See, for example, the description of elaborations and depth

of processing effects in Anderson, *Cognitive Psychology and Its Implications,* pp. 178–218.

19. Seminal basic research on strategy training has been conducted by Ann Brown, now of the University of California at Berkeley, and her colleagues. See for example: A. L. Brown, J. D. Day, and R. S. Jones, "The Development of Plans for Summarizing Texts," *Child Development* 54 (1983): 968–979; A. L. Brown and S. S. Smiley, "The Development of Strategies for Studying Texts," *Child Development* 49 (1978): 1076–1088; A. L. Brown, S. S. Smiley, and S. Q. C. Lawton, "The Effects of Experience on the Selection of Suitable Retrieval Cues for Studying Text," *Child Development* 49 (1978): 829–835. A summary of strategy training research with learning-disabled children, and some cautions concerning it, may be found in Laurie DeBettencourt, "Cognitive Strategy Training with Learning Disabled Students," in Patricia Myers and Donald Hammill, *Learning Disabilities: Basic Concepts, Assessment Practices, and Instructional Strategies,* 4th ed. (Austin, Tex.: Pro-Ed, 1990), pp. 453–467. See also a review by H. L. Swanson, "Strategy Instruction: Overview of Principles and Procedures for Effective Use," *Learning Disability Quarterly* 12 (1989): 3–14. In general, strategy training should not be conducted on tasks that are extraneous to schoolwork (games, for example), but should guide the children in dealing with their actual assignments.

20. S. Farnham-Diggory, *Schooling* (Cambridge: Harvard University Press, 1990).

21. Useful summaries of this research may be found in three special series commissioned by the *Journal of Learning Disabilities.* I refer here only to the introductory article of each series. Lee Swanson, "Information Processing Theory and Learning Disabilities: An Overview," *Journal of Learning Disabilities* 20 (1987): 3–7; Joseph Torgesen, "The Cognitive and Behavioral Characteristics of Children with Learning Disabilities: An Overview," *Journal of Learning Disabilities* 21 (1988): 587–589; Bernice Wong, "Basic Research in Learning Disabilities: An Introduction to a Special Series,"

Journal of Learning Disabilities 21 (1988): 195. Extensive review articles covering material through 1985 may be found in S. J. Ceci, ed., *Handbook of Cognitive, Social, and Neuropsychological Aspects of Learning Disabilities* (Hillsdale, N.J.: Erlbaum, 1986).

5 / NEUROPSYCHOLOGICAL RESEARCH

1. H. Hecaen and M. L. Albert, *Human Neuropsychology* (New York: Wiley, 1978).
2. Barbara Novick and Maureen Arnold, *Fundamentals of Clinical Child Neuropsychology* (Philadelphia: Grune & Stratton, 1988).
3. Andrew Ellis and Andrew Young, *Human Cognitive Neuropsychology* (London: Erlbaum, 1988).
4. Alexander Luria, *Higher Cortical Functions in Man* (New York: Basic Books, 1966).
5. Michael Cole, preface to Donna Vocate, *The Theory of A. R. Luria* (Hillsdale, N.J.: Erlbaum, 1987).
6. Luria, *Higher Cortical Functions*, p. 45.
7. Ibid., p. 239.
8. The Luria-Nebraska tests are available from Western Psychological Services, 12031 Wilshire Blvd., Los Angeles, CA 90025.
9. See, for example, Luria, *Higher Cortical Functions*, pp. 58–65.
10. See David Geary and Jeffrey Gilger, "The Luria-Nebraska Neuropsychological Battery–Children's Revision: Comparison of Learning Disabled and Normal Children Matched on Full Scale IQ," *Perceptual and Motor Skills* 58 (1984): 115–118; Daniel Nolan, Thomas Hammeke, and Russell Barkley, "A Comparison of the Patterns of the Neuropsychological Performance in Two Groups of Learning Disabled Children," *Journal of Clinical Child Psychology* 12 (1983): 22–27; Jeffrey Snow and George Hynd, "A Multivariate Investigation of the Luria-Nebraska Neuropsychological Battery–Children's Revision with Learning-Disabled Children," *Journal of Psychoeducational*

Assessment 3 (1985): 101–109; Jeffrey Snow, George Hynd, and Lawrence Hartlage, "Differences between Mildly and More Severely Learning Disabled Children on the Luria-Nebraska Neuropsychological Battery–Children's Revision," *Journal of Psychoeducational Assessment* 2 (1984): 23–28; Michael Tramontana and Stephen Hooper, "Child Neuropsychological Assessment: Overview of Current Status," in *Assessment Issues in Child Neuropsychology*, ed. Michael Tramontana and Stephen Hooper (New York: Plenum, 1988).

11. Charles Golden, "The Luria-Nebraska Children's Battery: Theory and Formulation," in *Neuropsychological Assessment and the School-Age Child: Issues and Perspectives*, ed. C. W. Hynd and J. E. Obrzut (New York: Grune & Stratton, 1981).

12. M. Passler, W. Isaac, and G. Hynd, "Neuropsychological Development of Behavior Attributed to Frontal Lobe Functioning in Children," *Developmental Neuropsychology* 1 (1986): 349–370.

13. Sally Springer and Georg Deutsch, *Left Brain, Right Brain* (New York: Freeman, 1989).

14. Ibid., chap. 2. Many additional references are listed in that chapter, which provides a readable overview of a very complex field.

15. Jerre Levy and Colwyn Trevarthen, "Metacontrol of Hemispheric Function in Human Split Brain Patients," *Journal of Experimental Psychology: Human Perception and Performance* 2 (1976): 299–312; S. Farnham-Diggory and Lee Gregg, "Color, Form, and Function as Dimensions of Natural Classification: Developmental Changes in Eye Movements, Reaction Time, and Response Strategies," *Child Development* 46 (1975): 101–114.

16. G. Geffen, J. Bradshaw, and G. Wallace, "Interhemispheric Effects on Reaction Time to Verbal and Nonverbal Visual Stimuli," *Journal of Experimental Psychology* 87 (1971): 415–422; D. Kimura, "Spatial Localization in Left and Right Visual Fields," *Canadian Journal of Psychology* 23 (1969): 445–458; A. Young and A. Ellis, "Different Methods of Lexical Access for Words Presented in the Left and Right

Visual Hemifields," *Brain and Language* 24 (1985): 326–358. This research has become sophisticated and complex. For a comprehensive review, see Christine Chiarello, "Lateralization of Lexical Processes in the Normal Brain: A Review of Visual Half-Field Research," in *Contemporary Reviews in Neuropsychology,* ed. Harry Whitaker (New York: Springer-Verlag, 1988).

17. D. Kimura, "Functional Asymmetry of the Brain in Dichotic Listening," *Cortex* 3 (1967): 163–178; F. W. K. Curry, "A Comparison of Left-Handed and Right-Handed Subjects on Verbal and Nonverbal Dichotic Listening Tasks," *Cortex* 3 (1967): 343–352; D. Kimura, "Left-Right Differences in the Perception of Melodies," *Quarterly Journal of Experimental Psychology* 16 (1964): 355–358.

18. Thomas Bever and R. J. Chiarello, "Cerebral Dominance in Musicians and Non-Musicians," *Science* 185 (1974): 537–539; P. R. Johnson, "Dichotically Stimulated Ear Differences in Musicians and Nonmusicians," *Cortex* 13 (1977): 385–389.

19. Merrill Hiscock and K. J. Bergstrom, "The Lengthy Persistence of Priming Effects in Dichotic Listening," *Neuropsychologia* 20 (1982): 43–53; Merrill Hiscock and Marcel Kinsbourne, "Asymmetries of Selective Listening and Attention Switching in Children," *Developmental Psychology* 16 (1980): 70–82.

20. Marcel Kinsbourne and R. E. Hicks, "Mapping Cerebral Functional Space: Competition and Collaboration in Human Performance," in *Asymmetrical Function of the Brain,* ed. Marcel Kinsbourne (Cambridge: Cambridge University Press, 1978); Marcel Kinsbourne and Merrill Hiscock, "Asymmetries of Dual-Task Performance," in *Cerebral Hemisphere Asymmetry,* ed. J. B. Hellige (New York: Praeger, 1983).

21. Marcel Kinsbourne and J. McMurray, "The Effect of Cerebral Dominance on Time Sharing Between Speaking and Tapping by Preschool Children," *Child Development* 46 (1975): 240–242.

22. Merrill Hiscock and Marcel Kinsbourne, "Specialization of

the Cerebral Hemispheres: Implications for Learning," *Journal of Learning Disabilities* 20 (1987): 130–143. This is a succinct overview of the methodological and theoretical issues. Readers who want to examine research reports in detail can begin with the 170 references in this article. For further overviews, summaries, and reference lists, see Marcel Kinsbourne, ed., "Brain Basis of Learning Disabilities," a special issue of *Topics in Learning and Learning Disabilities* 3 (1983).

23. John Obrzut, George Hynd, and Ann Obrzut, "Neuropsychological Assessment of Learning Disabilities: A Discriminant Analysis," *Journal of Experimental Child Psychology* 35 (1983): 46–55.

24. John Obrzut et al., "Effect of Selective Attention on Cerebral Asymmetries in Normal and Learning Disabled Children," *Developmental Psychology* 17 (1981): 118–125.

25. Marcel Kinsbourne, "Models of Learning Disability," *Topics in Learning and Learning Disabilities* 3 (1983): 1–13.

26. Hiscock and Kinsbourne, "Specialization of the Cerebral Hemispheres," pp. 138–139.

27. Elizabeth Warrington and Tim Shallice, "The Selective Impairment of Auditory Verbal Short-Term Memory," *Brain* 92 (1969): 885–896; Tim Shallice and Elizabeth Warrington, "Independent Functioning of Verbal Memory Stores: A Neuropsychological Study," *Quarterly Journal of Experimental Psychology* 22 (1970): 261–273.

28. Elizabeth Warrington, Valentine Logue, and R. T. C. Pratt, "The Anatomical Localisation of Selective Impairment of Auditory Verbal Short-Term Memory," *Neuropsychologia* 9 (1971): 377–387.

29. Tim Shallice and Elizabeth Warrington, "The Dissociation Between Short-Term Retention of Meaningful Sounds and Verbal Material," *Neuropsychologia* 12 (1974): 553–555.

6 / A DYSLEXIC BOY GROWS UP

1. "Dave" is of course a pseudonym, and neither the name of his examiner nor the locale can be revealed. However,

all quotations are from actual records and I have been very careful to maintain the authenticity of this case.

2. Numerous examples may be found in Uta Frith, ed., *Cognitive Processes in Spelling* (New York: Academic Press, 1980).

3. Laura Rothstein, "Section 504 of the Rehabilitation Act: Emerging Issues for Colleges and Universities," *Journal of College and University Law* 13 (1986): 229–265.

4. Anna Gillingham and Bessie Stillman, *Remedial Training for Children with Specific Disability in Reading, Spelling and Penmanship* (Cambridge: Educators Publishing Service, 1987).

5. Beth Slingerland, *A Multi-Sensory Approach to Language Arts for Specific Language Disability Children* (Cambridge: Educators Publishing Service, 1981).

6. Romalda Bishop Spalding and Walter T. Spalding, *The Writing Road to Reading* (New York: William Morrow, 1986).

7. A great deal of current research concerns the role of spelling in teaching children to read. The leader in this work is Linnea Ehri of the University of California at Davis. A summary of her work may be found in Linnea Ehri, "Movement into Word Reading and Spelling: How Spelling Contributes to Reading," in *Reading and Writing Connections*, ed. J. Mason (Boston: Allyn & Bacon, 1988). An example of Ehri's careful research is Linnea Ehri and L. S. Wilce, "Does Learning to Spell Help Beginners Learn to Read Words?" *Reading Research Quarterly* 18 (1987): 47–65. Recently, Ehri has taken the strong position that reading disability can be caused by failure to base instruction on the cognitive processes of spelling. See Linnea Ehri, "The Development of Spelling Knowledge and Its Role in Reading Acquisition and Reading Disability," *Journal of Learning Disabilities* 22 (1989): 356–365. Independently, Uta Frith, of the Cognitive Development Unit of the Medical Research Council in England, has worked out a compelling theoretical model of the interaction of reading and spelling in normal and dyslexic development: Uta Frith, "Beneath the Surface of Developmental Dyslexia," in *Surface Dyslexia: Neuropsychological and Cognitive Studies of Phonological*

Reading, ed. K. Patterson, J. Marshall, and M. Coltheart (Hillsdale, N.J.: Erlbaum, 1985). See also J. Morton, "An Information-Processing Account of Reading Acquisition," in *From Reading to Neurons,* ed. Albert Galaburda (Cambridge: MIT Press, 1989). I would like to point out that fifty years ago, Romalda Spalding discovered on a purely trial-and-error basis that spelling was the "road to reading." A feisty lady, Mrs. Spalding has been warring ever since with the reading establishment. Science may yet catch up to her remarkable intuitions.

8. Diana Hanbury King has published an extensive series of materials through the Educators Publishing Service, Inc., 75 Moulton St., Cambridge, MA 02238-9101.

9. Fortunately, Dave and other handicapped individuals who were protected during the school years by P.L. 94-142, and during the college years by Section 504 of the Rehabilitation Act of 1973, now also have the employment protection of the Americans with Disabilities Act, a law passed on July 26, 1990, that prohibits job discrimination against qualified disabled workers. This is considered the most important civil rights legislation since the Civil Rights Act of 1964. The definition of disability includes "any mental or psychological disorders such as mental retardation, organic brain syndrome, emotional or mental illness, or specific learning disabilities." A record of such impairment (such as Dave's college classification) is sufficient to establish it legally. Employers are now legally prohibited from discriminating against someone like Dave because of his dyslexia, and are required to make reasonable accommodations for him, such as providing editorial assistance. Only a few years ago I was contacted by a former client, a dyslexic social worker, who was about to lose her job because her case reports, which had to go into court records, contained so many spelling and syntactical errors. Under the new law, her employer will not be permitted to fire her for that reason, but will be required to make such reasonable accommodations as providing her with a word processor which includes a spell-checker and making pro-

visions for an assistant or colleague to proofread her reports before they are forwarded to the court.

10. A number of great men are reported to have been dyslexic, or at least to have had what we would now call a learning disability. These include Thomas Edison, Woodrow Wilson, Hans Christian Andersen, and Leonardo da Vinci. These historical claims, like all historical claims, are subject to rules of evidence and may be disputed. See Kimberly Adelman and Howard Adelman, "Rodin, Patton, Edison, Wilson, Einstein: Were They Really Learning Disabled?" *Journal of Learning Disabilities* 20 (1987): 270–279, and P. G. Aaron, Scott Phillips, and Steen Larsen, "Specific Reading Disability in Historically Famous Persons," *Journal of Learning Disabilities* 21 (1988): 523–545. Some of these cases are unquestionably authentic and can serve as inspirations for us all.

7 / RESEARCH ON DYSLEXIA

1. Although I am featuring the work of Breitmeyer and Lovegrove, for reasons of parsimony, there is an extensive additional body of research into visual processes of reading and dyslexia. For a general overview, see the *Journal of Experimental Psychology: Human Perception and Performance* 7 (1981), which is devoted to visual perception in reading. It includes a paper by David Badcock and William Lovegrove, "The Effects of Contrast, Stimulus Duration, and Spatial Frequency on Visible Persistence in Normal and Specifically Disabled Readers," pp. 495–505, and a number of other papers which, though not all addressing dysfunctional print processing, suggest where such dysfunctions might be located. Other research specifically addressing defective visual processing in dyslexics includes: Scott Blackwell, Curtis McIntyre, and Michael Murray, "Information Processed from Brief Visual Displays by Learning-Disabled Boys," *Child Development* 54 (1983): 927–940; H. Bouma and Ch. P. Legein, "Foveal and Parafoveal Recognition of Letters and Words by Dyslexics and by Aver-

age Readers," *Neuropsychologia* 16 (1977): 69–80; Julie Brannan and Mary Williams, "Allocation of Visual Attention in Good and Poor Readers," *Perception and Psychophysics* 41 (1987): 23–28; M. Clifton-Everest, "Dyslexia: Is There a Disorder of Visual Perception?" *Neuropsychologia* 14 (1976): 491–494; N. C. Ellis and T. R. Miles, "Dyslexia as a Limitation in the Ability to Process Information," *Bulletin of the Orton Society* 27 (1977): 72–81; Brenda Eskenazi and Sidney Diamond, "Visual Exploration of Non-Verbal Material by Dyslexic Children," *Cortex* 19 (1983): 353–370; Vincent Di Lollo, Dawn Hanson, and John McIntyre, "Initial Stages of Visual Information Processing in Dyslexia," *Journal of Experimental Psychology: Human Perception and Performance* 9 (1983): 923–935; E. R. Howell, G. A. Smith, and G. Stanley, "Reading Disability and Visual Spatial Frequency Specific Effects," *Australian Journal of Psychology* 33 (1981): 97–102; George Grosser and Carol Spafford, "Perceptual Evidence for an Anomalous Distribution of Rods and Cones in the Retinas of Dyslexics: A New Hypothesis," *Perceptual and Motor Skills* 68 (1989): 683–698; and Gordon Stanley and Rodney Hall, "Short-Term Visual Information Processing in Dyslexics," *Child Development* 44 (1973): 841–844.

2. Bruno Breitmeyer, "Sensory Masking, Persistence, and Enhancement in Visual Exploration and Reading," in *Eye Movements in Reading*, ed. Keith Rayner (New York: Academic Press, 1983); Bruno Breitmeyer, *Visual Masking: An Integrative Approach* (New York: Oxford University Press, 1984).

3. Table 10 is adapted from p. 232 of William Lovegrove, Frances Martin, and Walter Slaghuis, "A Theoretical and Experimental Case for a Visual Deficit in Specific Reading Disability," *Cognitive Neuropsychology* 3 (1986): 225–267.

4. Figure 18 is from Bruno Breitmeyer, "Unmasking Visual Masking: A Look at the 'Why' Behind the Veil of the 'How,'" *Psychological Review* 87 (1980): 52–69.

5. Figure 19 is also from Breitmeyer, "Unmasking."

6. Lovegrove, Martin, and Slaghuis, "A Theoretical and Experimental Case." See also Roberta Winters, Robert Patter-

son, and William Shontz, "Visual Persistence and Adult Dyslexia," *Journal of Learning Disabilities* 22 (1989): 641–645. These two articles include many additional references to the technical literature in this field.

7. Alvin M. Liberman, "Reading Is Hard Just Because Listening Is Easy," in *Wenner-Gren Symposium Series 54: Brain and Reading*, ed. C. von Euler, I. Lundberg, and G. Lennerstrand (London: Macmillan, 1989).

8. Alvin M. Liberman and I. G. Mattingly, "A Specialization for Speech Perception," *Science* 243 (1989): 489–494.

9. I. J. Gelb, *A Study of Writing* (Chicago: University of Chicago Press, 1963).

10. B. A. Blachman, "Phonological Awareness and Word Recognition: Assessment and Intervention," in *Reading Disorders: A Developmental Language Perspective*, ed. A. G. Kamhi and H. W. Catts (San Diego: College-Hill Press, 1988); L. Bradley and P. E. Bryant, "Categorizing Sounds and Learning to Read—A Causal Connection," *Nature* 301 (1983): 419–142; L. Bradley and P. E. Bryant, *Rhyme and Reason in Reading and Spelling* (Ann Arbor: University of Michigan Press, 1985); A. Content et al., "Accelerating the Development of Phonetic Segmentation Skills in Kindergartners," *Cahiers de Psychologie Cognitive* 2 (1982): 259–269; I. Lundberg, J. Frost, and O. P. Petersen, "Effects of an Extensive Program for Stimulating Phonological Awareness in Preschool Children," *Reading Research Quarterly* 23 (1988): 263–284; M. M. Rapala and S. Brady, "Reading Ability and Short-Term Memory: The Role of Phonological Processing," *Reading and Writing: An Interdisciplinary Journal* 2 (1990): 1–25; K. E. Stanovich, "Explaining the Variance in Reading Ability in Terms of Psychological Processes: What Have We Learned?" *Annals of Dyslexia* 35 (1985): 67–96.

11. Joseph Torgesen, "Studies of Children with Learning Disabilities Who Perform Poorly on Memory Span Tasks," *Journal of Learning Disabilities* 21 (1988): 605–612. See also R. K. Wagner and J. K. Torgesen, "The Nature of Phonological Processing and Its Causal Role in the Acquisition of Reading Skills," *Psychological Bulletin* 101 (1987): 192–

212. Torgesen makes the important point in this paper that lack of phonological awareness may be only one manifestation of a basic problem in phonological processing.

12. Figure 20 is from Torgesen, "Studies," p. 607.

13. Joseph Torgesen, "Cross-Age Consistency in Phonological Processing," in *Phonological Processes in Literacy,* ed. S. Brady and D. Shankweiler (Hillsdale, N.J.: Erlbaum, 1991).

14. I. Lundberg, "Lack of Phonological Awareness—A Critical Factor in Developmental Dyslexia," in *Wenner-Gren Symposium Series 54.*

15. K. Patterson, J. Marshall, and M. Coltheart, eds., *Surface Dyslexia: Neuropsychological and Cognitive Studies of Phonological Reading* (Hillsdale, N.J.: Erlbaum, 1985).

16. A good introduction to this complex clinical literature is Andrew Ellis and Andrew Young, *Human Cognitive Neuropsychology* (Hillsdale, N.J.: Erlbaum, 1988), esp. chaps. 7 and 8. In addition to Patterson, Marshall, and Coltheart, *Surface Dyslexia,* the following books describe numerous cases: M. Coltheart, K. Patterson, and J. Marshall, *Deep Dyslexia* (London: Routledge & Kegan Paul, 1980), and M. Coltheart, G. Sartori, and R. Job, *The Cognitive Neuropsychology of Language* (Hillsdale, N.J.: Erlbaum, 1987).

17. Albert Galaburda, Glenn Rosen, and Gordon Sherman, "The Neural Origin of Developmental Dyslexia: Implications for Medicine, Neurology, and Cognition," in *From Reading to Neurons,* ed. Albert Galaburda (Cambridge: MIT Press, 1989); Walter Kaufmann and Albert Galaburda, "Cerebrocortical Microdysgenesis in Neurologically Normal Subjects: A Histopathologic Study," *Neurology* 39 (1989): 238–244. Galaburda's research program originated in collaboration with the late Norman Geschwind, a distinguished neurologist whose interest in dyslexia began in the early 1960s and continued throughout his career. See, for example, Norman Geschwind, *Selected Papers on Language and the Brain* (Boston: Reidel, 1974), and Norman Geschwind and Albert Galaburda, "Cerebral Lateralization: Biological Mechanisms, Association, and Pathology," *Archives of Neurology* 42 (1985): 428–459, 521–552, 634–654.

18. Norman Geschwind and P. O. Behan, "Left-Handedness: Association with Immune Disease, Migraine, and Developmental Learning Disorder," *Proceedings of the National Academy of Science* 79 (1982): 5097–5100; Richard Olson et al., "Specific Deficits in Component Reading and Language Skills: Genetic and Environmental Influences," *Journal of Learning Disabilities* 22 (1989): 339–348; S. D. Smith, W. J. Kimberling, B. F. Pennington, and H. A. Lubs, "Specific Reading Disability: Identification of an Inherited Form through Linkage Analysis," *Science* 219 (1983): 1345–1347.

19. Gordon Sherman, Glenn Rosen, and Albert Galaburda, "Animal Models of Developmental Dyslexia: Brain Lateralization and Cortical Pathology," in Galaburda, *From Reading to Neurons.*

20. Albert Galaburda, "The Pathogenesis of Childhood Dyslexia," in *Language, Communication and the Brain,* ed. F. Plum (New York: Raven Press, 1988); Albert Galaburda, "Ordinary and Extraordinary Brain Development: Anatomical Variation in Developmental Dyslexia," *Annals of Dyslexia* 39 (1989): 67–80; Norman Geschwind, "Why Orton Was Right," *Annals of Dyslexia* 32 (1982): 13–30.

21. Margaret Livingstone, Glenn Rosen, Frank Drislane, and Albert Galaburda, "Physiological and Anatomical Evidence for a Magnocellular Defect in Developmental Dyslexia," *Proceedings of the National Academy of Science* 88 (1991): 7943–7947. See also Sandra Blakeslee, "Study Ties Dyslexia to Brain Flaw Affecting Vision and Other Senses," *New York Times,* September 15, 1991.

8 / SPATIAL AND MATHEMATICAL DISABILITIES

1. Elizabeth Warrington, "Constructional Apraxia," in *Handbook of Clinical Neurology,* vol. 4: *Disorders of Speech, Perception, and Symbolic Behaviour,* ed. P. J. Vinken and G. W. Bruyn (New York: Elsevier).

2. Peter van Sommers, *Drawing and Cognition: Description and Experimental Studies of Graphic Production Processes* (New York: Cambridge University Press, 1984); "A System for

Drawing and Drawing-Related Neuropsychology," *Cognitive Neuropsychology* 6 (1989): 117–164.

3. Further documentation is provided by another book in the Developing Child series: Jacqueline Goodnow, *Children Drawing* (Cambridge: Harvard University Press, 1977).

4. The precise areas of damage are shown in M. Vanier and D. Caplan, "CT Scan Correlates of Surface Dyslexia," in *Surface Dyslexia,* ed. K. E. Patterson, J. C. Marshall, and M. Coltheart (Hillsdale, N.J.: Erlbaum, 1985). Further details of L.B.'s case are in J. Derouesne and M.-F. Beauvois, "The 'Phonemic' Stage in the Non-Lexical Reading Process: Evidence from a Case of Phonological Alexia," in the same volume.

5. L. I. Benowitz, K. L. Moya, and D. N. Levine, "Impaired Verbal Reasoning and Constructional Apraxia in Subjects with Right Hemisphere Damage," *Neuropsychologia* 28 (1990): 231–241.

6. Neil O'Connor and Beate Hermelin, "Visual Memory and Motor Programmes: Their Use by Idiot-Savant Artists and Controls," *British Journal of Psychology* 78 (1987): 307–323. The reason for using such widely disparate age groups was to match the groups on mental age, which is computed from chronological age and IQ score. This matching is standard experimental practice in research of this type. The talents of the idiot-savants are often characteristic of a disorder known as autism or, in the case of high-functioning autists, as Asperger's Syndrome. For an extremely informative book on this topic see Uta Frith, *Autism* (Cambridge, Mass.: Basil Blackwell, 1989).

7. A. R. Luria, *Human Brain and Psychological Processes* (New York: Harper & Row, 1966), pp. 91–92. The classification of the disorders as Type I, Type II, etc., is my nomenclature, not Luria's.

8. A. R. Luria, *Higher Cortical Functions in Man* (New York: Basic Books, 1966), p. 160.

9. R. Cohn, "Arithmetic and Learning Disabilities," in *Progress in Learning Disabilities* II, ed. H. R. Myklebust (New York: Grune & Stratton, 1971).

10. Luria, *Human Brain,* p. 422.

11. Ibid., pp. 454–456.
12. Ibid., p. 253.
13. Ibid., pp. 254, 257.
14. Herbert Ginsburg, *Children's Arithmetic*, 2nd ed. (Austin, Tex.: Pro-Ed, 1989), pp. 216–217.
15. Ginsburg, *Children's Arithmetic*, 1st ed. (New York: Van Nostrand, 1977), pp. 140–143.
16. Beate Hermelin and Neal O'Connor, "Spatial Representations in Mathematically and in Artistically Gifted Children," *British Journal of Educational Psychology* 56 (1986): 150–157.
17. Ibid., p. 155.
18. Byron Rourke, *Nonverbal Learning Disabilities: The Syndrome and the Model* (New York: Guilford Press, 1989); Herman Myklebust, "Nonverbal Learning Disabilities: Assessment and Intervention," in *Progress in Learning Disabilities*, vol. 3, H. R. Myklebust, ed. (New York: Grune & Stratton, 1975).
19. For example, Mary Baratta-Lorton, *Mathematics Their Way* (Reading, Mass.: Addison-Wesley, 1976).

9 / CLASSIFICATION AND PLACEMENT

1. Erin Bigler, "Neuropathology of Acquired Cerebral Trauma," *Journal of Learning Disabilities* 20 (1987): 458–473. This article introduces a special series published by the *Journal of Learning Disabilities*, an excellent summary of contemporary research.
2. Ibid.; see p. 460.
3. Serge Duckett and Myron Winick, "Malnutrition and Brain Dysfunction," in *Brain Dysfunction in Children*, Perry Black, ed. (New York: Raven Press, 1981); Diana Fishbein and Jerzy Meduski, "Nutritional Biochemistry and Behavioral Disabilities," *Journal of Learning Disabilities* 20 (1987): 505–512.
4. Richard Kascsak and Henryk Wisniewski, "Pathogenesis of Virus-Induced and Autoimmune Nervous System Injuries," in *Child Neurology and Developmental Disabilities*, Joseph French, Shaul Harel, and Paul Casaer, eds. (Baltimore:

Grookes, 1989); Martin Kleiman and David Carver, "Central Nervous System Infections," in Black, *Brain Dysfunction in Children.*

5. Norman Geschwind and P. Behan, "Left-Handedness: Association with Immune Disease, Migraine, and Developmental Learning Disorders," *Proceedings of the National Academy of Science* 79 (1982): 5097–5100.

6. Abraham Towbin, "Perinatal Brain Damage and Its Sequels," in Black, *Brain Dysfunction in Children.*

7. S. D. Smith et al., "Specific Reading Disability: Identification of an Inherited Form through Linkage Analysis," *Science* 219 (1983): 1345–1347.

8. S. Farnham-Diggory and Billie Nelson, "Microethology of Spelling Behavior in Normal and Dyslexic Development," in *The Acquisition of Symbolic Skills,* Don Rogers and John Sloboda, eds. (New York: Plenum, 1983); Marcel Kinsbourne and Elizabeth Warrington, "Disorders of Spelling," *Journal of Neurology, Neurosurgery and Psychiatry* 27 (1964): 224–228; James Sweeney and Byron Rourke, "Neuropsychological Significance of Phonetically Accurate and Phonetically Inaccurate Spelling Errors in Younger and Older Retarded Spellers," *Brain and Language* 6 (1978): 212–225.

9. William Frankenberg and Jerry Harper, "States' Criteria and Procedures for Identifying Learning Disabled Children: A Comparison of 1981/82 and 1985/86 Guidelines," *Journal of Learning Disabilities* 20 (1987): 118–121.

10. C. R. Reynolds, "The Fallacy of 'Two Years below Grade Level for Age' as a Diagnostic Criterion for Reading Disorders," *Journal of School Psychology* 19 (1981): 350–358; C. R. Reynolds, "Measuring the Aptitude-Achievement Discrepancy in Learning Disability Diagnosis," *Remedial and Special Education* 6 (1985): 37–55.

11. Binet (1857–1911) was originally trained as a lawyer, and briefly attended medical school before finally settling on the (then) new science of psychology. Several of his early papers on child psychology have been republished in English by Robert Pollack and M. W. Brenner, eds., *The Experimental Psychology of Alfred Binet* (New York: Springer,

1969). They include experiments on children's reaction time, visual memory, perception of illusions, knowledge of word meanings, dreams, color perception, perception of length, and perception of numbers. In that work there are many ideas that were later made famous by Jean Piaget, who worked with Binet's successors in his laboratory from about 1919 to 1921. Binet wrote in 1908: "The child differs from the adult not only in the degree and quantity of his intelligence [the number of questions answered correctly], but also in its form [the quality of the answers]. What this childish form of intelligence is, we do not yet know. In our actual experiments we have only caught glimpses of it. It certainly demands careful study." (A. Binet, "The Development of Intelligence in Children," *L'Année Psychologique* XI, 1908.) Piaget apparently agreed, since he spent the next sixty years of his life studying exactly that.

12. Alfred Binet and Theodore Simon, "The Development of Intelligence in Children," in *Significant Contributions to the History of Psychology, 1750–1920*, ed. D. N. Robinson (Washington: University Publication of America, 1977).

13. For additional information about the history of intelligence tests, their misuse politically, new views of intelligence, and the role of intelligence tests in the classification of children as learning-disabled, see Raymond Fancher, *The Intelligence Men: Makers of the IQ Controversy* (New York: Norton, 1985); Howard Gardner, *Frames of Mind: The Theory of Multiple Intelligences* (New York: Basic Books, 1983); Stephen Jay Gould, *The Mismeasure of Man* (New York: Norton, 1981); Paul McDermott et al., "Core Profile Types in the WISC-R National Sample: Structure, Membership, and Applications," *Psychological Assessment: A Journal of Consulting and Clinical Psychology* 1 (1989): 292–299; Alan Kaufman, *Intelligent Testing with the WISC-R* (New York: Wiley, 1979); Keith Stanovich, "Discrepancy Definition of Reading Disability: Has Intelligence Led Us Astray?" *Reading Research Quarterly* 26 (1991): 7–29; and Robert Sternberg, *The Triarchic Mind: A New Theory of Human Intelligence* (New York: Viking Press, 1988).

14. Standard scores are calculated by taking a child's raw

score on an achievement test and transforming it mathematically into a number that expresses the child's deviation from the average. A standard score of 100 is the average. The IQ is also a standard score. (An IQ of 100 is average.) A standard score on an achievement test can therefore be compared directly to the IQ.

15. The Passage Comprehension section of the Woodcock-Johnson is a "fill in the blank" type of test, formally known as a *closure* test. For example: "On a shelf of a rocky mountain, the eagles had built their nest. Secure on the shelf, the nest would always _____ warm and dry." Words such as *be, remain,* or *stay* would be scored as correct. It is by no means clear how dyslexic readers deal with such tasks, nor why they improve with age and practice. There are several current research programs specifically addressing the issue of comprehension in dyslexia. P. G. Aaron, for example, has recommended that dyslexia be diagnosed in part by comparing reading comprehension to listening comprehension: P. G. Aaron, *Dyslexia and Hyperlexia* (Dordrecht, Netherlands: Kluwer Academic, 1989). Keith Stanovich has proposed that dyslexics can be distinguished from "garden-variety poor readers" by the specificity of the reading disorder. The garden-variety poor reader is, to use the language of Hinshelwood's case, "all-round poor," whereas the dyslexic is not. Keith Stanovich, "Explaining the Differences between the Dyslexic and the Garden-Variety Poor Reader: The Phonological-Core Variable-Difference Model," *Journal of Learning Disabilities* 21 (1988): 590–612.

16. S. Farnham-Diggory, *Schooling* (Harvard University Press, 1990). This book contains information about the changes afoot and how to help them along.

Credits

Figs. 1 and 2: Heinz Werner, "Development of Visuo-Motor Performance on the Marble-Board Test in Mentally Retarded Children," *Journal of Genetic Psychology* 64 (1944). Published by Heldref Publications, 1319 18th St., NW, Washington, D.C. 20036-1802. Copyright 1944. Reprinted by permission.

Fig. 3: Samuel T. Orton, *Reading, Writing, and Speech Problems in Children* (New York: Norton, 1937).

Fig. 4: Samuel T. Orton, "'Word-Blindness' in School Children," *Archives of Neurology and Psychiatry* 14 (1925): 581–615. Copyright 1925, American Medical Association.

Fig. 5: Newell C. Kephart, *The Slow Learner in the Classroom* (Westerville, Ohio: Merrill, 1971).

Figs. 6 and 7: Marianne Frostig, "Visual Perception, Integrative Functions, and Academic Learning," *Journal of Learning Disabilities* 5 (1972): 1–15. Copyright 1972 by the Donald D. Hammill Foundation. Reprinted by permission.

Figs. 8 and 9: Samuel A. Kirk and Winifred D. Kirk, *Psycholinguistic Learning Disabilities: Diagnosis and Remediation* (Champaign, Ill.: University of Illinois Press, 1971).

Fig. 11: H. Lee Swanson, "The Effects of Central Processing Strategies on Learning Disabled, Mildly Retarded, Average, and Gifted Children's Elaborative Encoding Abilities," *Journal of Experimental Child Psychology* 47 (1989).

Figs. 12, 13, and 14: A. R. Luria, *Higher Cortical Functions in Man* (New York: Basic Books, 1966).

Fig. 15: Sally P. Springer and Georg Deutsch, *Left Brain, Right Brain*, 3rd ed. (New York: W. H. Freeman, 1989). Copyright

Fig. 16: Elizabeth Warrington, Valentine Logue, and R. T. C. Pratt, "The Anatomical Localisation of Selective Impairment of Auditory Verbal Short-Term Memory," *Neuropsychologia* 9 (1971). Copyright 1971, Pergamon Press, Inc. Reprinted by permission.

Figs. 18 and 19: Bruno Breitmeyer, "Unmasking Visual Masking: A Look at the 'Why' behind the Veil of the 'How,'" *Psychological Review* 87 (1980). Copyright 1980 by the American Psychological Association. Reprinted by permission.

Fig. 20: Joseph Torgesen, "Studies of Children with Learning Disabilities Who Perform Poorly on Memory Span Tasks," *Journal of Learning Disabilities* 21 (1988): 605–612. Copyright 1988 by the Donald D. Hammill Foundation. Reprinted by permission.

Figs. 24, 25, and 26: Peter van Sommers, "A System for Drawing and Drawing-Related Neuropsychology," *Cognitive Neuropsychology* 6 (1989).

Figs. 27 and 28: Neil O'Connor and Beate Hermelin, "Visual Memory and Motor Programmes: Their Use by Idiot-Savant Artists and Controls," *British Journal of Psychology* 78 (1987).

Fig. 29: R. Cohn, "Arithmetic and Learning Disabilities," in H. R. Mykelbust, ed., *Progress in Learning Disabilities II* (New York: Grune & Stratton, 1971).

Fig. 30: Beate Hermelin and Neil O'Connor, "Spatial Representations in Mathematically and in Artistically Gifted Children," *British Journal of Educational Psychology* 56 (1986).

Tables 1 and 2: Judith Singer and John Butler, "The Education for All Handicapped Children Act: Schools as Agents of Social Reform," *Harvard Educational Review* 57 (1987): 125–152. Copyright © 1987 by the President and Fellows of Harvard College. All rights reserved.

Table 10: William Lovegrove, Frances Martin, and Walter Slaghuis, "A Theoretical and Experimental Case for a Visual Deficit in Specific Reading Disability," *Cognitive Neuropsychology* 3 (1986).

Index